LUNCHTIME MILLIONAIRE

LUNCHTIME MILLIONAIRE

A Step-by-Step Guide to Building Wealth...

On Your Lunch Hour

Didier Perennez

LUNCHTIME MILLIONAIRE,

PRINTED AND BOUND IN THE UNITED STATES OF AMERICA,

First Edition: September 2004

ISBN 0-9759676-0-6

10 9 8 7 6 5 4 3 2 1

Contents

CHAPTER FOUR

Choosing Your Financial Tools

CHAPTER FIVE

Where to Trade

CHAPTER SIX

CHAPTER SEVEN

CHAPTER EIGHT

CHAPTER NINE

CHAPTER TEN

Introduction

Historically, the stock market has been a safe and stable investment tool, with relatively few blips on the screen. With the notable exceptions of the market crashes of 1929 and 1987, for the greater part of the 20th century, conservative and moderate level investors could feel relatively safe parking their money in blue chip stocks, mutual funds, and index funds, being reasonably assured that their investment portfolios would steadily increase in value for many years to come. The sentiment on Wall Street encouraged buying and holding for the long term because it worked—the strategy was considered a near sure thing.

That world has changed. As we've crossed the threshold into the new millennium, we've witnessed corporate scandals that have not only rocked the stock prices of the firms involved, but that have had a tremendous effect on the stability of the market as a whole. We've witnessed major scrutiny over the manner in which some financial analysts have disseminated information over the years. Fears of biased reporting and conflicts of interest have left small investors wondering whom and what information they can really trust.

To compound matters, the world has become smaller. With the advent of the Internet, service jobs formerly held by U.S. citizens are being outsourced to other countries. Unprecedented threats of terrorism, security fears, and concerns over trade agreements and social security funds have combined to cause many of us to experience insecurity and doubt about our financial futures. These concerns are reflected in the way we live our lives and in the manner in which we invest.

Since the fall of the stock market in March 2000, a large number of investors have seen their holdings cut in half or worse, in many cases. Despite the worries and lingering negative sentiments, many investors are optimistic, continuing to believe in the long-term stability of the stock market. We have hope that things will turn around, that the return of reliability and profitability are just around the corner. Until recent years, most of us have lived only through bright times, never having experienced a prolonged drop in investment income.

What would happen, however, if the markets were to go flat for the next five to ten years? It has happened before. Would we be prepared for another prolonged slide? How many of us have a Plan B? How, as individual investors, can we predict if or when there will be another bull market? How can we determine if other major technological advances, comparable to the introduction of the personal computer and the Internet, will occur in the near future? And if these advances do come along, will they trigger the type of bull market we've seen in the past?

Neither you, I, nor any other investor can really be sure what the future holds. Even with this newfound uncertainty, however, there are still many opportunities to make money in the stock market. The individual investor simply needs to be adaptable to new methods and to employ fresh techniques. Gone are the days when we glanced at our portfolio statement once a month and collected our interest and dividends. Now we must be proactive. We need to apply some of the techniques that have been put into practice by the "big guys"—the institutional investors who have profited for decades from short-term strategies.

Institutional investors are typically investment firms, pension funds and life insurance companies. They pool funds from large numbers of individuals who have entrusted them to trade on their behalf. Because they are professional investors, they had exclusive access to the best resources and information for years. Now, thanks to the advent of high-speed Internet access and online trading systems, we can utilize many of the trading techniques that institutional investors use. Chief among these techniques is a strategy known as "momentum" trading.

Momentum trading has been practiced by institutional investors for many years, yet among private investors, it is rarely discussed. Traditionally, Wall Street has emphasized long-term investing for the majority of private individuals. Of course, long-term investing is an important part of every portfolio. Having a long-term strategy through a 401K plan, an IRA or mutual funds contributes greatly to your portfolio's financial stability and your own peace of mind. The downside is that long-term investing typically returns a yield of 10 percent per year on average or less over time.

What is momentum investing? Momentum investing is a short-term method of investing in the stock market that takes advantage of the rise and fall in individual stock prices over a relatively short period of time. Momentum investors typically hold their positions for anywhere from a few minutes to a few hours to a few days.

The *Lunchtime Millionaire* strategy uses momentum investing to buy stocks when they show signs of rising in price (upward momentum) and then sell them before they show signs of falling in price. Using relatively small amounts of money with each trade, *Lunchtime Millionaire* investors are able to steadily and consistently make conservative profits each week, thereby outperforming the typical long-term investments. Buying and selling stocks using momentum trading techniques sometimes allows you to increase your investment returns from the typical long-term yield of about 10 percent per year to up to 50 to 100 percent, or more, annually.

Let's take a look at a ten-year investment portfolio using long-term investments yielding 10 percent versus combined short- and long-term investments yielding 20 percent. If you invested $10,000 in 1990 at 10 percent annually, you would have approximately $26,000 by the year 2000, and approximately $67,000 by 2010. Twenty years after your initial investment, you'd have $67,000.

Now let's look at what that same $10,000 would yield if you used a combined short- and long-term investing approach to yield 20 percent. In ten years you would have $61,000, and in twenty years, your portfolio would increase to $380,000. While the 10 percent increase of $57,000 yield is certainly a substantial amount of money, consider this: Is it enough to take you and your family through your retirement years? By increasing your yield to 20 percent and your portfolio worth to $380,000 with a few short-term trades each week, you increase your family's security for years to come.

Savings, Retirement, and Beyond

How secure is your retirement? How certain are you of your ability to purchase a home? Consider a few statistics, courtesy of Robert

Brokamp of The Motley Fool, using data from the Congressional Research Service:

- The average Social Security benefit is less than $11,000 per year.

- On average, people retire with only $55,000 in savings. This, their "nest egg," is all they have to play with for the rest of their retirement days.

- To ensure a retiree doesn't outlive his or her savings, a maximum of 6 percent of the nest egg should be withdrawn per year. That's $3,300 per year in this case.

- This means the average retiree has only $14,300 a year in income ($11,000 + $3,300).

Frightening, isn't it? Unless you have a substantial savings account, your retirement years could be pretty lackluster. The activities you had planned, the trips you wanted to take, the hobbies you'd hoped to indulge, probably won't be possible at this income level. Even the comfort and security we look forward to in our old age may be at risk.

Many economic experts predict that as the baby boomers reach retirement, the social security funds in the United States will be heavily strained. We're now cautioned that we should be prepared to provide our own retirement savings, rather than rely on the social security system. It will be up to us to assure that our long-term plans and security are attained.

Perhaps you're not yet planning for retirement, but would like to realize your dream of buying a home. In November 2003, the National Association of Realtors reported that the average home price in America exceeded $177,000. In some states such as

California, however, the average home price exceeded $400,000. Even in two-income families that price can be prohibitive.

A New Wave of Investing

Starting in the mid 1990s, we began to see a new breed of investors emerging in the market—individuals who invest online via their personal computers and the Internet. These investors have begun to use the financial tools available on the World Wide Web/the Internet to conduct their own research and make their own decisions.

However, one of the impediments most online investors faced until recently was the difficulty of investing during market hours, because market hours typically coincide with working hours. Furthermore, many investors found it uncomfortable, or against company policy, to use the office computer for personal investing. The *Lunchtime Millionaire* strategy removes these limitations.

Whether you live in Seattle, Portland, San Francisco, or Las Vegas, you can now use a laptop computer and a wireless Internet connection to invest online at lunchtime. You can pick your potential winners while lounging at your favorite coffee shop, restaurant, or park, enjoying the convenience and simplicity of placing a few trades each week without taking time away from your work or pleasure. The *Lunchtime Millionaire* strategy allows you to maintain your regular schedule and paycheck, while achieving your income goals and fulfilling your retirement dreams.

CHAPTER ONE

The Overall Strategy

I have been thinking of writing this book for quite some time. It all started in 1996 when I realized I had come across a technique that would not only enable me to beat the major indices, but also surpass even the best performing mutual funds of the time.

When I first began investing, I was not interested in the high volume, high risk "day trading" that was becoming popular at the time. I wanted to find an investment strategy that was less risky and less complex, but still highly profitable. The technique I came across was momentum trading. Not only did it allow me to outperform my long-term investments, but it was a strategy that I, as a novice investor, felt comfortable engaging in.

With my laptop computer and an Internet connection (eventually a wireless connection), I began to place small, relatively conservative trades once or twice a week during my lunch break.

The late 90s were very profitable years for investors. The NASDAQ, where most technology companies trade, nearly doubled in 1999. It could be argued that anyone could have made money in those years. However, trading on the NASDAQ using my strategies, one can sometimes even make money during flat markets, and far more during good ones.

This book is an online-investing guide dedicated to individual investors who wish to increase their income with a limited amount of risk. It is not a book about day trading. It is about momentum trading with a focus on NASDAQ stocks. And it is about building wealth while you still need your day job.

If regular stock trading is so easy and so lucrative, why don't all individual investors do it? The answer is a simple one: fear—fear that they lack sufficient knowledge, fear that they'll pick the wrong stock, or fear that they'll fall victim to the kind of financial ruin prevalent during the infamous day trading years, the late 90s.

There are many misconceptions about trading. One is that you must be an investment professional, have a degree in finance or, at a minimum, have a great deal of knowledge about the financial markets. The truth is, none of these perceptions is true. Before I started trading, my knowledge of the market was limited to a handful of major companies such as IBM, Dell, and Microsoft. I built my knowledge gradually over the years, learning little by little every day.

For many people, the concept of trading seems complicated and difficult, not to mention risky. But times are changing. Do you recall the first time you made an online purchase using the Internet? You were probably more than a little hesitant as you typed in a slew of personal information and credit card numbers, sending them off into cyberspace.

But gradually, we all got used to the idea of buying online, and these days Internet buyers count in the millions, ranging from teenagers to senior citizens. It's my belief that, similarly, trading stocks on your own will soon become as common as purchasing a book on Amazon.com.

When you first begin to trade, it's natural to feel some fear. For this reason, I recommend investing only what you can afford. I recommend that you do not even invest real money at first, instead that you trade on paper. Then, when you're ready to get your feet wet, start small and gradually increase your trading funds over time. You might begin by allocating $2,000 to your trading portfolio and reinvesting funds only when you realize gains from trades. Starting small serves several purposes: It increases your comfort with trading, and it allows you to make mistakes at a level you can afford. If on the first time out, you make a mistake on a $1,000 trade, you'll be annoyed with yourself. But if you make a mistake on a $10,000 trade, you will be tempted to call it quits.

Also, remember that you can reach pretty substantive amounts even if you only start with $2,000. For example, a 3% daily average return on an initial investment of $2,000 at the beginning of the year takes you to $3.2 million by the end of the year (there are about 250 trading days in a year). Even investing at a daily average return as little as 2%, your $2,000 will become $280,000 by the end of the year – and that's after your $20/day buy and sell fees.

When first talking with clients and friends, I often hear statements like, "I don't know where to start," and "I don't have time to trade." This book will show you exactly where to begin, taking you step by step through the process:

1. Which computer and software are right for you

2. How to select a brokerage firm and commission plan

3. When to trade

4. Where to trade

5. How to trade

6. What strategies to use

7. Understanding the psychology of trading

As for the amount of time you'll need to devote to trading, it's entirely up to you. Whether you devote three hours every day or only three hours each month, you'll be moving in the right direction. On the days that you do trade, your trading activity will follow the pattern below:

- Twenty minutes in the morning will be spent investigating the most active stocks and their associated charts and news. You'll review the news on CNBC (a popular financial news channel that I will discuss later) and maybe place a trade or two.

- At lunchtime, you will allot twenty minutes to: examining the top twenty-five price percentage gainers on the NASDAQ, determining which stocks are potential winners, and maybe placing a trade or two.

- If you have the time, you'll spend twenty minutes tuning into evening television programs like "Lou Dobbs Tonight" and visiting a few message boards.

These time frames aren't written in stone; you will tailor them to your schedule. If your mornings are full and you can only devote time during your lunch hour, that is perfectly fine. You can spend as much or as little time trading as you like. Once you get involved in the markets, however, you'll likely find trading to be a fun, exciting hobby. And over time, as you continue to research and increase your trading, you'll find your comfort level approaching that of the experts.

CHAPTER TWO

Choosing Your Equipment

The first order of business in setting up your *Lunchtime Millionaire* system is to purchase a computer with Internet capability. Even if you already have a computer, please take a moment to read through this section. I've outlined a number of technical factors that you may not have considered and that may make your online investing experience more efficient and more enjoyable. In this chapter, we'll cover:

1. Computer requirements

2. Connecting to the Internet

3. Software requirements

4. Technical lingo

5. Troubleshooting

With new clients, I'm often asked the question, "Do I have to trade online with the *Lunchtime Millionaire* strategy, or can I use the phone to place orders?" The answer is that while placing orders online is not the only option, it's by far the best. Even though most brokerage firms allow you to place orders over the telephone, either with a real person or an automated system, the process is slow compared to online trading. Moreover, the automated version of phone trading doesn't allow you immediate access to the financial information you'll need to make the right investment decisions.

What about those cellular phones with Internet access? Unfortunately, even the more advanced cellular telephones don't currently provide the comfort that is important to a successful trading experience. And even the most sophisticated handheld computers are insufficient when it comes to reviewing many different pieces of information at the same time and at an optimal speed.

A laptop computer with a 15- or 17-inch viewable display is the optimal choice in equipment because it allows you space to display information from all of the various markets simultaneously and to achieve a feel for the markets as a whole. For example, a large screen with streaming real-time quotes allows you to monitor hundreds of stocks at once.

As you go about setting up your trading system, you'll encounter a great deal of confusing computer- and Internet-related jargon. Once you become familiar with these terms and their meanings, the purchasing process will be quite easy. But it can be intimidating in the beginning, so at the end of this section I've included a quick reference guide of frequently used hardware and Internet terms to assist you in making sense of it all.

1. YOUR COMPUTER

If your trading will be done from a location away from home or the office, you'll need to be mobile. You'll need a laptop computer. Thanks to the popularity of desktops and laptops in recent years, it is possible to purchase a fully functional laptop at a reasonable price (less than $1,000). Nowadays Internet capabilities and even wireless options are included or easily added.

Although you could theoretically achieve the same goals with any brand of computer, it is important to note that some software products that you may want to use down the line only run on Microsoft Windows-based computers (as of this writing). For this reason I strongly recommend a Microsoft Windows-based computer.

If you don't already have a laptop, you'll find a myriad of choices are available, from Dell to Hewlett-Packard to IBM. Be sure to pick a laptop that has a good CPU speed—between 1.5 GHz and 2.0 GHz. Memory is not usually an issue because 128 megabytes (MB), which is a minimum for most laptops these days, will suffice.

While the computer is not as critical as the quality of your Internet connection and the trading tools you choose, reliability is still extremely important. It goes without saying that a computer that frequently freezes, or has a weak battery, will cause frustration and time delays. In my experience, sticking with a major brand tends to pay off when it comes to a pleasant online investing experience.

Following are some of the minimum requirements you should look for in a computer:

Minimum Computer Requirements

Feature	Minimum Requirement
Processor (CPU) Speed	1.5 gigahertz
Operating System	Windows XP, 2000, or later
Central Memory (RAM)	128 megabytes
Display	15 inches
Hard-Drive Space	10 gigabytes
Battery Life	3 hours

2. YOUR INTERNET CONNECTION

Like your computer, the most important requirement of your Internet connection is that it be extremely reliable. As an active trader you can't afford disruptions of the signal just as you're about to hit the send button on a trade. Once again, choosing a major Internet provider tends to reduce the likelihood of service interruptions.

Before I talk about the various types of Internet connections available, let's take an overall look at the way in which you and your computer talk to the brokerage houses and exchanges each time you place a trade.

In illustration 2.1, you can see that when you place a trade through your computer, a signal is sent to your wireless Internet provider, which passes that signal, via the Internet, along to your brokerage house. Your brokerage house then communicates directly with the appropriate exchange in order to place the trade. After the trade is executed, the exchange notifies your brokerage house, which sends you an electronic confirmation. It continues to amaze me that the whole process happens within just a few seconds. Later on, we'll discuss trade execution in depth. For now, let's focus on how the message containing your trade gets from one point to another.

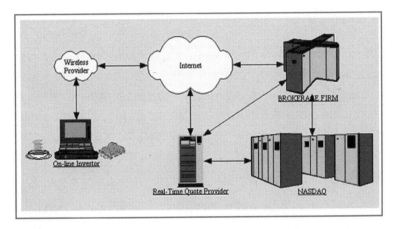

Illustration 2.1

There are four different ways to connect to the Internet:

1. Wi-Fi (wireless fidelity)

2. 3G Wireless

3. Dial-up

4. Cable

5. DSL (Digital Subscriber Line)

When subscribing to any of these wireless services, be sure to inquire as to how much data transfer you will be allowed per month. Just as your cell phone company charges you overage fees when you exceed your allotted minutes, wireless service providers often charge overage fees for the total amount of data transferred above and beyond that provided by your plan. Some plans, however, offer unlimited access, which I highly recommend.

Wi-Fi

When it comes to wireless connections, there are quite a few options available. My personal favorite is the wireless Wi-Fi technology, available through many Internet providers. Wi-Fi is technically called IEEE 802.11b. The advantage of Wi-Fi is that it provides Internet speeds comparable to those of a DSL or cable modem. Because of its speed and portability, Wi-Fi is becoming the hottest wireless technology available.

Compared to cellular technology (the technology developed for cellular phones, which allows electronic signals to be carried over many miles), Wi-Fi technology transmits electronic signals only about 50 feet. As of this writing, you must be physically close to an antenna (called an access point) to receive the signal. The reward for being close to an access point is an amazingly high connection speed. While we can anticipate that the range will increase beyond 50 feet in the future, for now it should be adequate given where you'll find yourself trading.

Most access points are currently available in airports, coffee shops such as Starbucks, and some restaurants. As Wi-Fi's transmission range increases, it will most likely be available in sites not associated with particular restaurants or cafés, but on a neighborhood basis.

The technology is now available through T-Mobile (www.tmobile.
com) and a few other companies, one of with whom you will
need to set up an account in order to access its network. T-Mobile
offers a variety of plans starting at approximately $29 a month for
unlimited access, with 500 megabytes of data transfer included.

If you are uncertain which Wi-Fi company to sign up with, call
the restaurant or coffee shop where you plan to trade most often

and ask if it has a Wi-Fi access point and, if so, which company
it subscribes to. You can then sign up for wireless service with the
same company.

In addition to setting up a Wi-Fi account, you will need to acquire a
Wi-Fi-compatible PC Card (also called a PCMCIA card) for your
laptop, similar to the one shown here. Many laptops already come
pre-equipped with Wi-Fi, so check your manual or configuration
if you are unsure.

If your laptop is not pre-equipped with Wi-Fi (for example, if it
doesn't have built-in wireless technology, like Intel's Centrino),
you'll know if it does), you'll need to buy a PC card, which costs
less than $100. Once your PC card is inserted and your Wi-Fi
account enabled, you can start using your high-speed Internet
access at any remote location that is close to an access point.

When using Wi-Fi, you must use the wireless service available at the particular restaurant or coffee shop where you decide to trade. This can create a dilemma if you trade at various locations that subscribe to different wireless providers. For example, if you trade at Starbucks, you'll need to subscribe to T-Mobile to access their Wi-Fi access points. If you go down the street to trade at a café that uses the Deep Blue network, you'll need to subscribe to Deep Blue.

There is a solution to this problem, however. In addition to subscribing to your favorite location's wireless provider, you can also subscribe to a regular wireless account, which, while slower than Wi-Fi, provides access nearly everywhere. You'll then have the best of both worlds—fast access via Wi-Fi and extensive coverage via regular wireless.

3G WIRELESS

Otherwise known as "third generation," 3G wireless is a technology that allows you to trade virtually anywhere, regardless of the service provided by the venue in which you want to trade. Since 3G service utilizes some of the same technology as your cell phone service, you can typically receive 3G service anywhere you receive wireless phone service.

In terms of geographic signal coverage, Wi-Fi probably won't compete with 3G wireless for quite some time. The companies providing cell phone usage have had many years to establish their networks, while Wi-Fi is just beginning its expansion.

On the other hand, 3G wireless is still slow compared to Wi-Fi. Instead of a speed of one megabit (1,000 kilobits) per second (which you get with Wi-Fi), 3G wireless transmits only 56, or sometimes 128, kilobits per second. This is similar to comparing DSL and cable to dial-up: a ratio of at least 10 to 1 in terms of speed. I do anticipate that 3G wireless will eventually increase its speed but, at this point, it still has a ways to go.

Subscribing to this type of wireless service is similar to opening up a cell phone account, and can be done through a variety of companies such as Sprint, Verizon, or T-Mobile at a price in the neighborhood of $35 per month. You will need a PC card as well, although a different type than the PC Card used for Wi-Fi service. PC Cards compatible with 3G are priced at approximately $200, and have a small, protruding antenna. They can be purchased from any of the companies from which you purchase your wireless service.

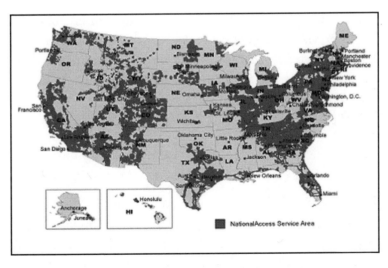

Chart 2.2 3G national wireless coverage as of January 2003.

DSL/CABLE

No Internet discussion would be complete without some mention of DSL and cable Internet connections. Perhaps you belong to the growing population of people who work from home, whether as a consultant or as a regular employee, and plan to do much of your trading from home. If your needs for mobility are limited, DSL or cable may be an option for you.

At a price of around $39 per month, DSL is becoming more affordable, and is available in an increasing number of cities. If DSL is not available where you live, it is likely that cable is. Cable offers connection speeds similar to DSL, and both DSL and cable can be installed relatively quickly.

Most computers are capable of handling DSL or cable. Only a Network Interface Card (NIC) is required. In some instances, the NIC is provided as part of your subscription. The majority of new DSL users typically find installing their new systems a relatively easy and trouble-free task, since many DSL providers have self-installation instructions down to a science.

DIAL-UP

The majority of computer owners still connect to the Internet through dial-up, which typically offers speeds of 56 kilobits per second. This speed is very slow compared to DSL (as I mentioned before, about 10 times slower). Considering the widespread availability of high-speed Internet connections and the minimal difference in price, I strongly advise upgrading from your dial-up connection to a high-speed connection. It's one thing to send e-mail and to surf the Web with a dial-up connection, but when it comes to trading online, speed will increase your ability to execute your investment decisions properly.

In the chart below, you'll find comparisons of the various connection types, along with the reliability, speed, and cost of each.

Comparison of Internet Connection Methods:

Connection Type	Reliability	Speed	Cost
Dial-up (Ground)	Good	Slow	Inexpensive
3G (Wireless)	Good	Slow	Expensive
Wi-Fi (Wireless)	Excellent	Fast	Fairly Inexpensive
DSL/Cable (Ground)	Excellent	Fast	Inexpensive

Internet Connection Comparisons in Relative Speed to Dial-up:

Connection Type	Relative Speed
3G (Wireless)	1 to 2 times faster
Wi-Fi	27 times faster
DSL or Cable	27 times faster
Enhanced DSL	90 times faster

Each person will have a different level of trading activity, and different levels of services they will use when trading online. For some, particularly for less active traders, the expense of DSL or Wi-Fi may not make sense. However, for the active trader, DSL or Wi-Fi is nearly mandatory. To help you determine which Internet connection is appropriate for you, the following chart lists various trading activity levels, along with two types of quote systems, and recommended Internet connection options for each.

Of course, these are only recommendations, and you can always change your Internet connection if your trading activity level changes. Be sure to check with your provider to understand contract length, terms, and penalties before signing a contract.

Internet Connection Comparisons
Relative to Trading Activity and Services:

Trading Activity Level	With Streaming Real-Time Quotes + Charts	Without Real-Time Quotes
Very Active	DSL or Wi-Fi	DSL or Wi-Fi
Fairly Active	DSL or Wi-Fi	3G Wireless
Occasional	3G Wireless	3G Wireless

As I mentioned earlier, the optimal arrangement would be to subscribe to both Wi-Fi and 3G wireless. You'll use Wi-Fi when you are near an access point and enjoy the great connection speed. And when you are not near an access point, or need a backup system, you'll still have your 3G wireless service.

The primary factor to consider when choosing an Internet connection is whether you will be able to trade online if your Internet connection is slow. A true 56 kilobit-per-second connection is not particularly slow when you are primarily transferring numbers (as opposed to images). Much of online trading content is, in fact, numbers. Even stock charts are fairly lightweight. However, downloading Web pages from your brokerage firm's website can take time. If you start to experience more than a two second wait for a quote, or more than five seconds to retrieve a chart or a brokerage page, your connection is probably too slow.

3. YOUR SOFTWARE REQUIREMENTS

The software requirements of the *Lunchtime Millionaire* system are simple and relatively few. To get started, you'll need an Internet browser, which will give you access to most of the investment tools you'll be using, like quotes, news, and financial statements. Most computers come with Internet browsers such as Netscape Navigator or Microsoft Internet Explorer, already installed.

Another important aspect to consider is that Internet technology has evolved a great deal over the years and many investment and other websites now frequently include special features, features that your browser may or may not support. If you often get error messages such as "syntax error" or "script error" when attempting to visit the various investment websites, you will want to change Web browsers.

4. Technology Lingo Translations

For answers to your questions regarding any of the computer and Internet terms we've discussed above, please reference the following definitions and explanations, provided courtesy of Webopedia.com, with some additions.

WIRELESS TRANSFER: The process of transmitting and receiving data over the air waves.

TRANSFER RATE: The speed with which data can be transmitted from one device to another. Data rates are often measured in megabits (millions of bits) or megabytes (million of bytes) per second. These are usually abbreviated as Mbps and MBps, respectively. Another term for data transfer rate is throughput.

CONNECTION SPEED: The speed with which users download information from the Web or upload data to the Web.

BROWSER: Short for Web browser, a software application used to locate and display Web pages. The two most popular browsers are Netscape Navigator and Microsoft Internet Explorer. Both of these are graphical browsers, which means that they can display graphics as well as text. Most modern browsers can present multimedia information, including sound and video.

PCMIA CARD: Short for **P**ersonal **C**omputer **M**emory **C**ard **I**nternational **A**ssociation, and pronounced as separate letters, PCMCIA is an organization comprising some 500 companies, which has developed a standard for small, credit card sized devices, called *PC cards*. Originally designed for adding memory to portable computers, the PCMCIA standard has been expanded several times and is now suitable for many types of devices. There are, in fact, three types of PCMCIA cards. All three have the same rectangular size (85.6 by 54 millimeters), but different thicknesses.

Type I cards can be up to 3.3 mm thick, and are used primarily for adding additional ROM or RAM to a computer.

Type II cards can be up to 5.5 mm thick, and are often used for modem and fax modem cards.

Type III cards can be up to 10.5 mm thick, which is sufficiently large for portable disk drives.

As with the cards, PCMCIA slots also come in three sizes:

A Type I slot can hold a Type I card

A Type II slot can hold a Type II card or a Type I card

A Type III slot can hold a Type III card or any combination of two Type I and II cards.

In general, you can exchange PC cards on the fly, without rebooting your computer. For example, you can slip in a fax modem card when you want to send a fax and then, when you're done, replace the fax modem card with a memory card.

MEGABIT / MEGABYTE:

In decimal systems, the prefix *mega* means one million, but in binary systems, *mega* stands for 2 to the 20th power, or 1,048,576. One megabyte, therefore, is either 1,000,000 or 1,048,576 bytes (this is equivalent to 1,024K), depending on the context.

Since there are 8 bits in a byte, a megabyte is equivalent to 8 million bits. A bit is the smallest unit of memory in a computer.

KILOBIT: One thousand bits. Often used in "kilobits per second." In areas of the country where DSL and cable are not available, people use a regular modem (56 kilobits per second) to connect to the Internet.

NETWORK ADAPTOR or NIC:

Often abbreviated as *NIC*, an expansion board you insert into a computer so the computer can be connected to a network. Most NICs are designed for a particular type of network, protocol, and media, although some can serve multiple networks. Most computers today come with a built-in network adaptor.

INTERNET:

A global network connecting millions of computers. More than 100 countries are linked into exchanges of data, news, and opinions through the Internet.

Unlike online services, which are centrally controlled, the Internet is decentralized by design. Each Internet host, a computer system where websites are stored, is independent. Its operators can choose which Internet services to use and which local services to make available to the global Internet community. Remarkably, this anarchy by design works exceedingly well.

There are a variety of ways to access the Internet. Most online services, such as America Online, offer access to some Internet services. It is also possible to gain access through a commercial Internet Service Provider (ISP).

The Internet is **not** synonymous with the World Wide Web.

THE DIFFERENCE BETWEEN THE INTERNET AND THE WORLD WIDE WEB

Many people use the terms Internet and World Wide Web (a.k.a. the Web) interchangeably, but in fact the two terms are not synonymous. The Internet and the Web are two separate, but related, entities.

The *Internet* is a massive network of networks, a networking infrastructure. It connects millions of computers together globally, forming a network in which any computer can communicate with any other computer as long as they are both connected to the Internet. Information that travels over the Internet does so via a variety of languages known as protocols.

The *World Wide Web*, or simply the *Web*, is a way of accessing information through the medium of the Internet. It is an information-sharing model that is built on top of the Internet. The Web uses HTTP, only one of the protocols used over the Internet, to transmit data. Web services, which use HTTP to allow applications to communicate in order to exchange business logic, use the Web to share information. The Web also utilizes browsers, such as Internet Explorer and Netscape Navigator, to access Web documents called Web pages, which are linked to each other via hyperlinks. Web documents also contain graphics, sounds, text, and video.

The Web is just one of the ways that information can be disseminated over the Internet. The Internet, not the Web, is also used for e-mail, which relies on SMTP, Usenet news groups, instant messaging, and FTP (File Transfer Protocol). So the Web is just one portion of the Internet, albeit a large portion; the two terms are not synonymous and should not be confused.

5. Troubleshooting

We all have days when things just stop working. However, those little snafus can have a devastating effect when you're regularly trading online. It's critical that those days leave a minimal impact on your ability to make money in the stock market.

What do you do when you're in the middle of trading and things go wrong? Following is a simplified, yet targeted, troubleshooting guide that should help get you through the most common problems.

They fall into two categories:

1. Computer and Internet problems

2. Brokerage house problems

Computer and Internet Problems:

Beginning with the worst case scenario ...

Problem: Your computer is not booting (starting up).

Solution: If it doesn't appear that you are even getting to the point where the operating system is loading (when you see the Windows logo appear on the screen), turn the computer off. Wait 30 seconds, then turn it on again. Do this three times, if necessary.

If your computer is a laptop and still does not boot, make sure it is off then shake it *very* gently. Many times this will alleviate the problem, at least temporarily. There is such a concentration of components in today's laptops that sometimes when undesired connections occur, the computer fails to boot. Believe it or not, shaking it gently often gets things going until you have a chance to permanently fix the problem.

Problem: The computer is booting and the operating system is loading (you see the Windows logo on the screen), but an avalanche of error messages tells you that there is trouble. You might even get to the "log on" screen where you enter your username and password, but the picture doesn't look pretty.

Solution: At this point, you might consider two things: Enter your username and password and wait to see what happens next, or reboot using the <CTRL> <ALT> <DEL> keys simultaneously while depressing the F8 key. This will take you to a menu where you should choose *safe mode* option. The safe mode allows you to boot your computer in a mode in which none of the sensitive drivers will load. *Drivers* are software programs that control your network adapter, your video adapter, and other hardware add-ons, with the network and video drivers being the ones most likely to fail at start-up. Safe mode should allow you to logon and verify that your computer is not entirely dead. From that point, try a soft reboot (ALT-CTRL-DEL).

Problem: You're not able to connect to your wireless provider (no signal or the authentication fails).

Solution: First make sure your PCMCIA card is properly plugged in. Second, ask another user who might be using the same wireless provider if they are getting a signal. If not, the wireless service is likely down. You might then contact your wireless provider to see how long the outage is going to last. If your wireless provider's service is up and running, there may be one of two other potential problems: Either your PCMCIA card has been damaged, or your logon information is not recognized. In either case, your best bet is still to contact your wireless provider.

Problem: You seem to be able to connect to the Internet because you were able to log on to your wireless provider, but you can't browse any Web pages on the Internet (your brokerage account's website, Yahoo! quotes, etc.)

Solution: This is likely an outage at the level of your wireless provider, not in terms of its ability to deliver a signal to you, but in terms of its ability to connect to the Internet "backbone." In some rare instances, the problem might be the Internet backbone itself. Contact your wireless provider to find out which it is.

Brokerage House Problems:

Problem: You are definitely connected to the Internet. You can browse various websites, but you are unsuccessful in your attempts to enter or browse your brokerage account's website.

Solution: Continue trying to access the brokerage pages, as the server might be extremely busy, particularly when the markets are very active. On the other hand, it's quite possible that the brokerage's website is down. You might then consider placing your trades by phone instead. It's less efficient, but it works in a pinch.

When it comes to the actual placing of a trade online, there are some technical considerations to bear in mind. Did the trade go through? Was your stock executed at the right price? Here are the common problems that can occur when placing trades, along with steps you can take to solve them:

Problem: Your Internet connection failed, or your brokerage account's website went down, as you were placing a trade. As a result, you received a "Page not found" response or, in some rare cases, an "Access denied" response from your brokerage account's website.

Solution: There are two possibilities here. If the connection went down before the "Your order has been confirmed" page appeared then, in all likelihood, your order was not sent. Try re-establishing your Internet connection or, if it becomes clear that the problem lies with your brokerage site, try to place your trade later.

If the connection went down after you were forwarded to the order confirmation screen, it's likely that your order went through. The only way to verify this, however, is to re-establish the connection and then go to the "pending orders" or "portfolio" screen to see if your order appears.

Problem: You were trying to sell a losing stock and your order did not seem to go through.

Solution: First, don't panic. I've been in this situation a few times, and quite surprisingly, when I did re-establish my connection, I found that the stock had actually rebounded a bit. Of course, you win some, you lose some.

There will be times, however, when the stock does not rebound, and your instincts tell you it's not likely that it will in the near future (for example, in the case of a company announcing extremely bad news). Contact your brokerage firm by phone immediately to ask if the order went though. If it did not, you have little recourse. If you still feel negative about the company, your only option is to place your trade over the phone.

In either of these last two scenarios, it's important to be aware of a clause in all brokerage contracts that stipulates that the brokerage is not responsible for any financial losses you incur due to equipment failures (whether yours or theirs), market conditions, or other factors. These liability limitations are typically stated in the following manner:

Information and content herein is furnished as is without warranty, express or implied, including but not limited to fitness for a particular purpose, implied warranties of merchantability or non-infringement of third party rights, or freedom from computer viruses. In no event will [the brokerage house] or its affiliates be liable for any damages, including without limitation direct or indirect, special, incidental, or consequential damages, losses, or expenses arising in connection with this site or use thereof, or inability to use by any party, or in connection with any failure of performance, interruption, error, omission, defect, Access to services may be affected by market conditions or system performance.

You'll find that for the most part, your trading experience will be smooth and trouble-free. When system or market problems do occur, however, it is important not to allow yourself to be discouraged or frustrated. It's simply part of the process, so the best thing to do is to accept the situation and move on.

CHAPTER THREE

Choosing Your Brokerage

C hoosing an online brokerage house may seem like a relatively simple process, and in the case of an investor who places three or four trades per year, it is not critically important which brokerage he or she uses. Occasional traders don't typically accumulate large commission fees or qualify for frequent trading discounts or other perks that differentiate one brokerage house from another. As a frequent trader, however, those perks and commissions can really add up, so there are a number of factors you'll want to consider before placing that first trade.

If you've already been investing for some time, you probably have at least a rudimentary understanding of the various types of brokerage firms and the different types of accounts available for the individual investor. Features and services change rapidly in the brokerage industry, however, so this may be a good time to compare your existing brokerage firm's online services with those of its competitors. In this chapter I'll discuss the various types of brokerage firms, the different types of accounts they offer, and which features you'll want to subscribe to in order to take full advantage of the *Lunchtime Millionaire* strategy.

There are as many different types of brokerage accounts as there are investors, but they are typically broken down into two categories: 1) Traditional full service and 2) Discount. To get the greatest benefit from the *Lunchtime Millionaire* strategy, I highly recommend using a discount brokerage. The primary appeal of the traditional brokerage is that presumably you'll have an experienced investment professional guiding your decisions. One of the main thrusts of the *Lunchtime Millionaire* strategy, however, is that by acquiring knowledge gradually and safely, you will learn to make your own decisions. What's more, lower commission structures inherent in discount brokerages will help you keep your overhead costs down.

When choosing the right brokerage firm for you, there are a number of features and services you'll need to investigate. In this chapter I will describe them one by one:

1. Brokerage commissions

2. The markets in which you are allowed to trade

3. Execution speed and price

4. Trade limitations

5. Minimum deposit requirements

6. Types of accounts available

7. Advanced features

8. Ease of use

9. Customer service

After comparing the features of the various firms and narrowing your choices, be sure to check the background of the firms you are considering with the National Association of Securities Dealers (www.nasd.com), particularly if their names are not familiar to you. You can also check the popular website www.gomez.com, which provides up-to-date comparative data about each firm.

1. BROKERAGE COMMISSIONS

The commission you pay your broker when you buy or sell a stock is the first, and perhaps the most important, factor to consider when choosing a brokerage firm. Commissions can eat into your profits substantially, particularly for investors starting out with relatively small-dollar-value trades. Brokerage fees on individual trades can vary from $10 to $40 per trade.

Excitement over a $200 profit on a trade will quickly evaporate if $40 of those proceeds goes to the broker even before the cash has hit your account. After deducting another 40 percent or so for capital gains taxes, your previous $200 profit can decline to as little as $84. So finding a brokerage with a good commission structure is key.

Here's an example: If you purchased 200 shares of XYZ Corporation at $10 per share and a day later sold your position at $11 per share, you would have made a 10 percent profit on your investment in just one day. Sounds pretty appealing, doesn't it? Take a closer look at those numbers, and the difference a $20 versus a $30 commission can make:

Commission	$30	$20
Total Purchase Price	$2,000	$2,000
Total Selling Price	$2,200	$2,200
Gross Profit	$200	$200
Buying Commission	-$30	-$20
Selling Commission	-$30	-$20
Net Profit	$140	$160
Percentage Profit	7%	8%

While the difference between a $20 commission and a $30 commission may not seem to be worthy of lengthy analysis, consider this: You pay a commission each time you buy and each time you sell. There are approximately 250 trading days in a year in which, theoretically, you could place 250 buy and sell trades. That's $5,000 per year you'd lose by choosing a brokerage that charges $30 per trade instead of $20 per trade.

So why not just choose the brokerage firm with the lowest commission per transaction? Because there's yet one other factor to take into consideration when comparing commission fees. Many firms charge not only a flat fee per transaction, but also a per-share fee.

For example, ABC Brokerage may charge a very attractive fee of $5 per trade. However, that flat fee may only be good for trades of less than 500 shares. For trades in excess of 500 shares, you may be charged the $5 flat fee plus a fee for each share traded. These per-share fees can range anywhere from 2 cents per share up to as much as 10 cents per share. When you're trading large quantities of low-priced stocks, per-share fees can represent a large chunk of your total commissions. I highly recommend you choose a brokerage firm that charges only a flat fee for each trade.

Let's say you decide to purchase 2,000 shares of XYZ Corporation at $1 per share. One day later, you sell your position at $1.10 per share, resulting in a $200 profit. If you pay a flat fee of $30 per trade, your net proceeds would be $140. On the other hand, if you choose to pay a flat fee of $5 plus a 5 cent-per-share fee over 500 shares, your net profit would be $40. Quite a difference!

Take a look at the following comparison of fees:

	$30 Flat Fee	$5 Flat Fee + 5 cents/share over 500 shares
Total Purchase Price ($2000 shares at $1)	$2000	$2000
Total Selling Price	$2200	$2200
Gross Profit	$200	$200
Buying Commission	-$30	-$80 (= $5 + $0.05 x 1500)
Selling Commission	-$30	-$80
Net Profit	$140	$ 40
Net Percentage Profit	7%	2%

In addition to commission fees, be sure to read the fine print on annual account maintenance, check-writing fees, and fees to wire or transfer funds. Firms that charge fees for these types of services often have other hidden charges that will take you by surprise later on down the road. Before choosing a brokerage firm, therefore, it's a good idea to sit down and list the various services you might like to use.

In addition to commission and account fees, always inquire about frequent trader discounts. Many brokerage houses offer lower commission rates for investors who place more than 75 trades or so per month. Even if you don't trade with that frequency, some firms may grant you the discounted commission rate if you pay a monthly subscription fee.

Many brokerage firms also offer special promotions or perks for opening new accounts or depositing large sums of money into an existing account. These promotions may not be advertised or mentioned on the brokerage's main website, so be sure to call and ask about them.

2. THE MARKETS IN WHICH YOU ARE ALLOWED TO TRADE

There are three major stock exchanges in the United States: The New York Stock Exchange (NYSE), the American Stock Exchange (AMEX) and the NASDAQ.

With the advent of the Internet has come an increasing popularity in trading not only NYSE, AMEX, and NASDAQ stocks, but on various international exchanges and electronic quotation systems as well. A familiarity with these various exchanges and systems will help you in your consideration of a brokerage firm.

The NYSE

The well-established NYSE, www.nyse.com, has been an institution for more than one hundred years, and is increasingly considered the world's premier stock exchange. Companies listed on the NYSE comprise a wide variety of sectors, including utilities, manufacturing, insurance, finance, and technology, to name a few.

The most commonly used indicator of how the NYSE is fairing is the Dow Jones Industrial Average, known as the Dow. As of this writing, the Dow consists of NYSE stocks in the following sectors:

- Technology: 16%

- Healthcare: 13%

- Financial Services: 22%

- Consumer Discretionary and Service: 14%

- Retailers, casinos, hotels, film production, etc.

- Consumer Staples: 7.7%

- Utilities: 7%

- Transportation: 2.6%

- Integrated Oils: 4%

- Materials and Processing: 2.3%

The AMEX

The American Stock Exchange, www.amex.com, is a smaller stock exchange than the NYSE in terms of both volume and the number of listed companies, and typically lists smaller companies than those on the NYSE. The AMEX now operates under the umbrella of the NASD (National Association of Securities Dealers), which includes the NASDAQ. Stocks traded on the NYSE and AMEX exchanges are often referred to as "listed stocks."

The NASDAQ

The NASDAQ, www.nasdaq.com, was created in 1971 and has traditionally been the exchange of choice for technology companies. The NASDAQ is an electronic, or computerized, stock market and is, in my opinion, the most exciting of the three because of the profit potential of the companies it lists.

What exactly is an automated exchange? In exchanges such as the NYSE or AMEX, trades are handled by real people, located at stock exchange buildings. Trading occurs when specialists communicate with each other by calling out share quantities and prices of the companies in which they wish to trade.

The NASDAQ, on the other hand, is a newer, decentralized market in which geographically separate dealers are linked by computer screens. NASDAQ stocks are often referred to as OTC, or "over-the-counter" stocks, and their transactions are automated.

Nearly all brokerage firms allow their account holders to buy and sell stocks on any of these three major stock exchanges.

THE OTC BULLETIN BOARD AND THE PINK SHEETS

In addition to the NYSE, AMEX, and NASDAQ, there are two other exchanges of which you should be aware: the OTC Bulletin Board and the Pink Sheets.

The OTC Bulletin Board, or OTCBB, operates under the umbrella of NASD and represents great opportunities to invest in much smaller companies. The Pink Sheets is yet another category of electronic quotation systems. The Pink Sheets typically represents companies that either cannot meet the stringent qualification requirements of the larger exchanges such as the NYSE, the AMEX, the NASDAQ, or even the OTC Bulletin Board, or that cannot afford the expense of being listed on those exchanges.

In fact, many companies that have been "delisted" from the larger exchanges (due to instability or a consistently low stock price), will end up on the Pink Sheets or the OTC Bulletin Board. These firms are often called "microcaps" because of their much lower market capitalization ("market capitalization," or "market cap," meaning the number of shares outstanding multiplied by the price per share).

OTC Bulletin Board and Pink Sheets stocks typically represent a much higher risk level than what you would experience with stocks listed on the three majors. Hence, online investors typically stay away from these sometimes extremely volatile stocks until they become more comfortable with the level of risk involved (for a practical definition of the word "volatile," please refer to the glossary). On the other hand, it is fair to say that the returns can be substantially higher.

(For a detailed discussion of the risks and rewards of microcap stocks, visit this Web page from the Securities and Exchange Commission's website:

www.sec.gov/investor/pubs/microcapstock.htm

Contrary to what you may have heard, trading in OTC Bulletin Board and Pink Sheets stocks can be as easy as trading on the bigger and more well-known exchanges.

However, not all brokerage firms allow you to do so. For those that do, however, you'll find that the level of information available rivals those of the stocks on the major exchanges. The primary exception to that rule is that with the Pink Sheets, the bid price (the highest price at which investors are willing to buy) and the ask price (the lowest price at which investors are willing to sell) are substituted by the last price information (the price at which the stock was last bought or sold).

Many brokerage firms allow Pink Sheets trading in much the same manner and quality of trade execution as listed stocks. However, on the OTC Bulletin Board or the Pink Sheets, stocks are sometimes sporadically traded. This means trading volume may alter between very heavy and very light. It can, therefore, sometimes be more difficult to buy and sell these stocks when you want to.

INTERNATIONAL SECURITIES

Finally, if you have an interest in international companies, you may want to be sure the brokerage house you choose enables you to trade in foreign stocks. While some international companies trade only on foreign exchanges, many also trade on U.S. exchanges.

In these cases, the stocks are known as American Depository Receipts, or ADRs.

There are brokerage firms that specialize specifically in global markets, providing excellent research and coverage, even allowing you to trade using U.S. currency. The popularity of ADRs has increased dramatically in recent years, and placing a percentage of your portfolio in foreign markets can be one way of increasing your diversification.

OTHER INSTRUMENTS

I'm frequently asked by investors whether they can use the *Lunchtime Millionaire* strategy to invest in such instruments as bonds, currencies, options, and futures. I have only applied the strategy to stocks and I suggest you do the same. That said, there is certainly no reason why these other instruments can't be part of your portfolio.

3. EXECUTION SPEED AND PRICE

The second factor you'll want to include in your brokerage firm comparison is the speed at which trades are executed. What exactly is execution, and how does it affect your trade? To best understand execution, it's helpful to take a look at what happens to your order after you've hit the send button on your computer. Following is a scaled down version of the trip your buy or sell order takes as it winds its way through the execution process.

Each time you buy or sell a stock, your order is sent from your computer to your brokerage house. An automated system within your brokerage house then determines where to send the trade from there. For a NASDAQ stock, it may be sent to an electronic communication network (connecting buyers and sellers directly) or to a middleman called a market maker. A market maker is a broker that specializes in specific stocks. Market makers hold large quantities of particular stocks in inventory, thereby guaranteeing that interested investors can buy them.

Some brokerage houses have special relationships or agreements with market makers. In situations such as these, the discount brokerage typically routes the majority of its trades through the market maker with whom they are aligned.

For stocks traded on the NYSE, your trade may also be routed from your brokerage house to an electronic communications network. However, if it's a larger trade, it may be sent directly to a specialist on the floor of the exchange. How quickly your trade is then executed (or completed), depends on the technology and routing processes of your brokerage firm.

What's the difference between a market maker and a specialist? Market makers deal with NASDAQ stocks, while specialists deal with stocks that trade on the NYSE.

THE TECHNOLOGY OF YOUR BROKERAGE FIRM

Let it be said that when it comes to technology, not all firms are created equal. Surprisingly, some of the largest firms may have old servers (the powerful computers that process trades and store financial information), and those old servers are simply not as fast as the newer ones.

Differences in brokerage firms' technologies become important when placing frequent trades, particularly in a rapidly moving market. While the variations in the speed of trade executions among the various firms are usually no more than three or four seconds, those few seconds count tremendously when it comes to the price at which your trade is executed, particularly when the market is moving quickly.

Let's say that you turn on your computer one morning and see that the Federal Reserve has lowered interest rates. The market is reacting to the news with a huge jump in volume as investors clamor to buy. You see that Dell is trading at $52 per share, and decide to place an order of your own.

If your brokerage firm has fast, advanced technology, within two or three seconds you'll own Dell stock at $52 per share. If your brokerage firm's technology is slow, your order may instead be placed in four or five seconds, when Dell may already be at $53 per share. That scenario will compound if you place a limit order, in which case your order may not get filled at all (I will discuss limit orders in detail in chapter 9).

Current and reliable technology is critical. Unfortunately there is no way for the average investor to know how up-to-speed his or her brokerage firm is. Only experience will tell you that, and that means you have to place a few trades. It's not enough just to visit the firm's website and pull up a few quotes or news items.

Trades can be handled by different servers than those used for market or account information. One way to compare is to observe the amount of time that elapses between the time you place a trade and the time you receive a confirmation of your order. This should occur in a matter of two or three seconds, even with a low-speed Internet connection.

If you find you are consistently waiting five or more seconds for the confirmation page to pop up, chances are your brokerage firm's technology is not as advanced as it should be. Of course, there will be rare occasions when the actual backbone of the Internet is down, or times when trading conditions are extreme. During those times, the servers in many firms will experience delays. This, however, is rare. On an average trading day, your confirmation pages should appear almost immediately.

Gomez.com, a website I mentioned earlier, also ranks online brokerage firms by technical factors such as the length of time it takes to log in and the length of time it takes to place a trade. As of this writing, the online brokerage firms were ranked in the following order (with the best performing brokerage firm listed first):

Gomez.com Technology Rankings

1. Harris Direct

2. E*Trade

3. Ameritrade

4. Brown & Company

5. Fidelity

6. Charles Schwab

7. Scottrade

8. TD Waterhouse

4. TRADING LIMITATIONS

Brokerage firms often have a set limit of shares you can trade in any single transaction. These limits vary widely from firm to firm, and range anywhere from 1,000 to 5,000 shares per transaction. The majority of the time, you'll find that share limit range to be quite adequate. However, it can cause problems if you are an investor with an interest in smaller stocks.

Let's say, for example, you like to follow companies such as Amazon.com (stock symbol: AMZN). On one particular day, Amazon was trading at $20 per share. If your brokerage firm's trading policy limits you to 500 shares per transaction, you can safely purchase $10,000 worth of Amazon. For most novice traders, a $10,000 limit is far more than enough.

If, however, you become interested in a company like Sun Microsystems (SUNW), which as of this writing is trading at $3 per share, you will be limited to a $1,500 investment. That could be restrictive even for the novice trader. If you plan to buy more than 500 shares of SUNW, you'll have to place more than one trade. And remember, with some brokerage houses, a commission fee applies on a per transaction basis, in addition to any per-share fees you incur.

Of course, this is not meant to imply that I recommend placing large amounts of money into any one single security. There are times, however, when you feel confident enough with your research to place large block trades for shares of a company. On those occasions, you'll feel frustrated if you're limited by the number of shares you can place at one time, particularly when the market is moving quickly and time is of the essence.

5. Minimum Deposit Requirement

Most brokerage houses require a minimum level of cash as a deposit in order to open an account. For example, many online brokers require that you deposit a minimum of $1,000 to $2,000 to open a new account. While $1,000 to $2,000 is considered reasonable, if you shop around, you may find even lower minimums through special promotions. Some brokerage firms that offer more advanced features and services may require a larger deposit, often in the range of $5,000 or more, to get started.

Once your account is open, some brokerages might charge fees if you fail to trade on a regular basis, or if you let the cash on deposit in your account fall below a certain level. These fees may be referred to as "inactivity" or "minimum deposit" fees. It's a good idea to determine these deposit and activity requirements ahead of time, and to try to find a firm that best suits your planned trading activity and cash level.

6. Types of Accounts Available

There are a few types of accounts that nearly all brokerage houses offer: the "Cash" account and the "Margin" account. Beyond those two types of accounts, you'll find a wide array of specialized accounts and services. But in this section, we'll deal primarily with cash and margin accounts.

CASH ACCOUNTS

A cash account is the most common type of account, and requires that you have the full amount of cash, or funds, in your account when you purchase a security.

MARGIN ACCOUNTS

A margin account, on the other hand, allows you to borrow from the brokerage firm to finance your purchases.

Even though some people feel comfortable trading on margin, I highly recommend opening a cash account, at least initially. Many people have gotten into debt with margin accounts. This is because, unlike a cash account, with a margin account you can potentially lose not only the money you've invested, but much more.

You see, one of the requirements of margin borrowing is that the value of the cash or collateral stocks must equal as much as 50 percent of the new stocks you purchase on margin. During downturns in the market, collateral stocks may decrease in price, dipping below that required 50 percent level.

When this happens, you may receive what's known as a "margin call." To maintain the 50 percent ratio, your brokerage firm will request that you deposit cash into your account. If you do not have the cash to deposit, the brokerage is allowed to sell the stocks you used as collateral for your purchase. This can result in a substantial loss.

You may have heard about the tremendous numbers of margin calls in the stock market crash of October 1987, when the market slid more than 30 percent in just five days. That day, "Black Monday," and the days following it, had the largest weekly point loss in the history of the U.S. stock market. Many investors were forced to sell their holdings at huge losses to cover their margin calls.

To add insult to injury, within the next two years the market rebounded, and many stocks went back to their previously high price levels. If those investors who had succumbed to margin calls had had enough cash in their accounts to cover those margin calls, chances are they could have ridden out the crash instead of selling at a loss.

One beneficial feature of a margin account is that it allows you to "short" stocks. Shorting a stock is selling a stock you don't own, with the intent of buying it back at a future date at a lower price. How do you sell a stock you don't own? The answer is that the brokerage firm allows you to borrow the stock for a certain period of time.

While you are borrowing the stock, you can sell it, but you'll need to buy it back at a date in the future, usually within three months or so, in order to return it to the brokerage house. You're essentially betting that the price of the stock will go down, so that when you do purchase it, you can buy it back for less than you sold it. The risky part of short selling comes if the stock goes up, particularly if it goes up substantially, losses can be unlimited. That is why I never recommend short selling to novice investors.

For those readers who would like to experiment with margin investing, it's a good idea to explore the various types of margin accounts available. Margin accounts are typically divided into two levels. The first level, which I discussed above, allows you to purchase stocks valued at twice the amount of your collateral stocks. The second level of margin account allows you to purchase stocks valued at four times the value of your collateral stocks. The second level is typically only available to active traders in good standing.

7. Advanced Features

Some brokerage accounts offer additional advanced features, particularly to customers who trade frequently. For example, E*Trade offers a service called Power E*Trade, which provides a lower transaction fee for investors who meet certain trading volumes. Even investors who trade only once a day easily qualify for these lower fees. As an eligible online trader, the fees you pay for each trade may be as low as $10 (compared to $20), and you'll have access to valuable trading tools such as real-time streaming data.

Another benefit some brokerage houses offer frequent traders in good standing is the ability to trade immediately upon depositing funds in an account. Otherwise, you may have to wait until the check clears. Some brokerages may also allow frequent traders to use funds from the sale of a stock before that trade is fully completed (settled).

Normally, the Securities and Exchange Commission does not require a brokerage to give you access to the proceeds of your sell orders until after three days, when the sell has "settled." However, some brokerage firms will allow you to use the "unsettled" funds from a sale prior to that three-day period. Many firms require you to open a margin account with a minimum balance to take advantage of this capability. This is something you'll want to check into.

Also consider the rate at which you'll be paid interest on your cash balances. Most brokerage houses provide the option of sweeping any unused funds into a money market account. The interest on these accounts can vary up to a full percentage point, so be sure to compare rates. Some firms, such as E*Trade, also have an affiliated bank which pay even higher interest rates and often offer checking privileges. Transferring funds from the online investing division to the banking division is typically simple and convenient.

8. Ease of Use

While ease of use is not as critical as the commission rates or the speed of trade executions, a poorly designed online trading system can really put a damper on the enjoyment you derive from your trading experience. When evaluating the simplicity of your brokerage firm's online access, there are two primary pages to consider: the Account Balance page and the Trading page.

With the Account Balance page, be sure to compare the ease with which you can understand the numbers and key totals. For example, some firms list your buying power only on the Account Balance page, while others list it on the Trading page as well. Listing your buying power on the Trading page prevents you from having to flip from page to page when placing multiple trades, which saves you valuable time. In a hot market, every second counts.

You'll also want to assess the accuracy of the numbers on your Account Balance page. Are they up to date? As I discussed above, some firms allow you to use "unsettled" funds to purchase other stocks. How is this reflected? If you sell a stock in the morning and want to buy another at lunchtime, is it easy to determine whether or not those funds are available? Some firms include funds under the listing "buying power" that are not available for immediate use. Be sure you understand how various firms treat buying power and funds from unsettled trades or recent deposits.

Another aspect to consider is how frequently the firm updates its account information. For instance, some brokerage firms update the Account Balance page only once each day, while other firms update on a real-time basis. Because the Account Balance page lists your buying power, real-time updates are critical. When placing a trade, you want to be absolutely certain you have enough funds in your account. If those figures are not included on a real-time basis, you may have to resort to your memory and a calculator to keep abreast of your buying power.

A final factor to consider is the hours during which you'll be allowed to trade. Most online brokerages offer trading during three time periods: Pre-opening, from 5 to 6:30 A.M. (PST); regular market hours, from 6:30 A.M. to 1 P.M. (PST); and after hours, from 1 to 5 P.M. (PST). Be sure your brokerage conforms to those hours as well.

9. CUSTOMER SERVICE

Many discount brokerages have an online presence only, with no physical branches. While this can often save you money in commissions, it can be frustrating if you want to deposit funds immediately or talk over the phone with a representative. While Charles Schwab (also called "Schwab") has many physical branches, E*Trade has just recently begun establishing them.

It also is important to determine how easy it is to reach brokerage representatives on the phone and how knowledgeable they are. I've had a number of instances when a trade went through incorrectly, and being able to reach an informed, helpful agent was critical in resolving the issue. Beware of the brokerage house that puts you on hold for fifteen minutes or more. Be sure also to ask about its hours of operation. A reputable discount brokerage firm should maintain customer service hours in the range of approximately 7 a.m. to midnight (EST).

In terms of overall rankings, as of this writing Gomez.com rates discount brokerages in the following order based on ease of use, customer confidence, on-site resources, relationship services, and overall cost:

Gomez.com Customer Service Rankings

1. Fidelity Investments

2. Charles Schwab

3. E*Trade

4. Harris Direct

5. TD Waterhouse

6. Wells Trade

7. Ameritrade

8. Cititrade

9. American Express Brokerage

10. T. Rowe Price Brokerage

Rankings change from time to time, so be sure to visit <u>Gomez.</u> <u>com</u> for the most recent listings. Also remember that you may place a higher value than Gomez does on a particular feature (for example, the size of commissions), so you'll want to take your own needs and preferences into account. Most of the top online brokerage firms offer excellent service, so as long as you choose one within the top ten, you shouldn't be disappointed.

CHAPTER FOUR

Choosing
Your Financial Tools

After you've chosen your equipment and your brokerage firm, you'll want to become accustomed to the various investment tools that will help you in your research and decisions. In this chapter, I'll focus on the most useful sources of financial information, as well as the most helpful websites about online trading.

Choosing the right investment tools will be essential in making your trading experience a convenient, pleasurable one. The sources of information described here are not only the most reliable and informative, they're ones I use and find indispensable.

REAL-TIME QUOTES

You may have, at one time or another, visited Yahoo! Finance or one of a number of other websites where stock prices are displayed.

Many of these financial websites contain free stock prices on a 15- or 20-minute delayed basis, which typically serves the purposes of long-term investors fairly well.

Short-term investing, however, requires a more extensive set of services on a real-time basis. The first and most important of these tools is real-time quotes. This is a tool you won't want to be without, as any savings you might realize on delayed quotes can be a fraction of what you stand to lose by not being on top of the market.

Let's take a look at a real-life example. On May 5th, FSI International (FSII), a stock I had been watching, showed a sharp increase in its stock price for the second day in a row. When, on the second day, the stock dropped from its peak of $2.85 per share to $2.75 in the last 20 minutes of trading, I placed a buy order. Within 10 minutes, the stock rebounded to $2.85, a 3.5 percent increase, at which point I sold the position.

Had I not had access to real-time quotes, I would have missed the drop and the subsequent rebound. By the time I would have noticed the price fluctuation, the market would already have closed and my buy/sell opportunity would have passed. While a 3.5 percent increase may not seem like much, it is precisely the type of profit you are looking for when you trade on a conservative, short-term basis.

Chart 4.1

Until recent years, real-time quotes cost a good deal of money. Nowadays, however, you can subscribe to real-time quote packages, charts, and stock monitoring capabilities through Yahoo! Finance and other sources for approximately $10 per month. When you use these tools, you will see that the numbers on your screen are updated constantly throughout the trading day. The number of stocks you can monitor for this price is very limited, however. You may want to check instead with your brokerage house. Many brokerages also are beginning to offer free or low-cost streaming quotes for those who qualify as frequent traders.

More comprehensive "premium" packages are available through companies like PC Quote. For $75 or more per month, PC Quote's package includes:

• Real-time streaming quotes

• Real-time charts

• Real-time news

- Most-active screens

- NASDAQ Level II (real-time access to best bid and ask prices from individual market makers)

- Technical analysis

These packages often include tools such as stock screeners, which allow you to sort bundles of stocks by volume, price, or percentage increase/decrease.

Here is a list of some companies that offer premium packages:

- Yahoo! Finance's "Real-Time" package

- Ameritrade's Streamer

- E*Trade's "Market Trader"

- Townsend Analytics' RealTick/PC Quote

Many brokerage houses do provide, free of charge, real-time quotes and the ability to program and monitor lists of real-time stock prices on your screen. However, these offerings are sometimes limited in terms of the number of stocks you can monitor, and it is necessary to hit the "refresh" button on your browser in order to update the prices. Stock prices that don't update dynamically are called "static quotes."

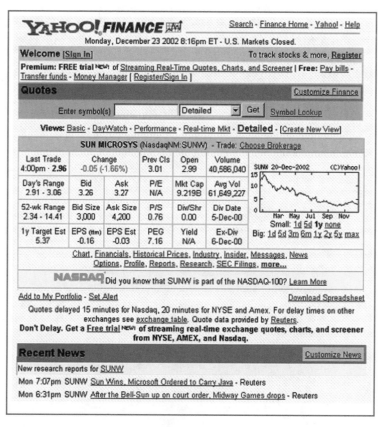

Chart 4.2 - Yahoo! Finance's Quote Screen

STOCK SCREENERS

Stock screeners are extremely useful when you are looking for stocks that belong to a given sector or industry. I often use screeners when I'm searching for potential Sympathy Plays, companies that operate in the same industry as a company that has just made the news (I discuss Sympathy Plays in depth in chapter 8). I also use stock screeners to acquaint myself with less familiar players in any given industry.

In addition to sorting by industry or sector, stock screeners allow you to sort by variables such as price, price earnings ratio, market capitalization, and analyst rating. The following graph illustrates a typical stock screener for a search of companies in the computer networks industry, with a share price between $5 and $10:

Screener Settings

Search for stocks by selecting from the criteria below. Click on the "Find Stocks" button to

Category

Industry:

| Any |
| Advertising (Services) |
| Aerospace & Defense (Capital Goods) |
| Air Courier (Transportation) |
| Airline (Transportation) |

Index Membership   Any

Share Data

Share Price:	Any	Min	Any	Max
Avg Share Volume:	Any	Min	Any	Max
Market Cap:	Any	Min	Any	Max
Dividend Yield:	Any	Min	Any	Max

Performance

| 1 Yr Stock Perf: | Any | |
| Beta (Volatility): | Any | Min | Any | Max |

Sales and Profitability

| Sales Revenue: | Any | Min | Any | Max |
| Profit Margin | Any | Min | Any | Max |

Valuation Ratios

Price/Earnings Ratio:	Any	Min	Any	Max
Price/Book Ratio:	Any	Min	Any	Max
Price/Sales Ratio:	Any	Min	Any	Max
PEG Ratio:	Any	Min	Any	Max

Analyst Estimates

Est. 1 Yr EPS Growth:	Any
Est. 5 Yr EPS Growth:	Any
Avg Analyst Rec:	Any
(1=Buy, 5=Sell)	

Results Display Setting

| Display info for: | Actively Screened | Data |

Chart 4.3 Stock Screener

Symbol	Company ▲	Industry	Index Mem	Retail Price	Avg. Vol	Market Cap	Div/Yld	Return %	Beta	Sales
ASIA	Asiainfo Holdings Inc	Computer Networks	N/A	6.64	333,090	293.40M	0.0%	-64.59	2.907	$135.31M
CMNT	Computer Network Technology	Computer Networks	N/A	7.01	442,045	187.89M	0.0%	-62.03	2.272	$210.65M
ELTE	ELITE Information Group Inc	Computer Networks	N/A	9.26	22,000	72.50M	0.0%	-25.92	0.954	$75.56M
LEON	LION Bioscience AG	Computer Networks	N/A	6.30	14,464	125.18M	0.0%	-59.35	1.858	$35.35M
LNOP	Lanoptics Ltd	Computer Networks	N/A	5.35	28,409	39.01M	0.0%	-17.31	1.451	$748,000
MEDW	Mediware Information Systems Inc	Computer Networks	N/A	8.51	15,545	61.99M	0.0%	110.64	0.437	$30.76M
RADS	Radiant Systems Inc	Computer Networks	S&P 600 SmallCap	8.90	48,772	248.89M	0.0%	-17.97	1.613	$137.34M
RSYS	Radisys Corp	Computer Networks	S&P 600 SmallCap	8.10	59,227	142.99M	0.0%	-59.50	2.767	$208.73M
RDWR	Radware Ltd	Computer Networks	N/A	8.00	70,772	132.44M	0.0%	-39.35	2.323	$41.06M
SNIC	Sonic Solutions	Computer Networks	N/A	5.23	313,681	86.14M	0.0%	-0.38	2.143	$25.80M

Chart 4.4 Results of Stock Screening.

MOST ACTIVES PAGES

Another investment tool I find indispensable is the Most Actives pages. These pages give you a feel for the stocks that are showing heavy activity in price or volume. Dramatic activity in price or volume can be caused by a variety of factors, such as extremely good or bad news, new product approvals or denials, high or low earnings, or rumors about any of those kinds of events. The rankings of the most active stocks on these pages are updated every few seconds throughout the trading day.

Because momentum trading focuses on taking advantage of movements in stock prices over the course of a relatively short time period such as an hour or a day, the most actives pages are an ideal place to start and/or finish your day. Once you analyze which stocks are moving or most likely to move, you can place your buy orders accordingly. I'll be discussing how you can use the most actives pages in your trading strategies at length in the pages to come.

The most actives pages are usually included in all premium quote packages available through companies such as Yahoo! Finance. The following image shows a typical result of a search for the most active stocks at a given point in time. Following the price, volume, and net change for each stock, you'll also find keys for retrieving news and charts—key information sources for finalizing your decision to buy or sell.

	Major U.S. Indices | Advances & Declines | **U.S. Most Actives**					
Volume Leaders: NASDAQ | AMEX | NYSE						
Price % Gainers: NASDAQ | AMEX | NYSE						
Price % Losers: NASDAQ | AMEX | NYSE					International: Europe	
Symbol	**Name**	**Last Trade**	**Change**		**Volume**	**Related Information**
AMRN	AMARIN CORP	1:47pm 4.739	+1.709	+56.40%	276,543	Chart, Messages, Profile, **more...**
IOMT	ISOMET CORP	1:33pm 2.16	+0.72	+50.00%	16,800	Chart, Messages, Profile, **more...**
GEMP	GEMPLUS INTL SA	1:31pm 2.735	+0.635	+30.24%	171,200	Chart, Messages, Profile, **more...**
VIRS	TRIANGLE PHARM	1:46pm 5.85	+1.35	+29.94%	14,775,621	Chart, Messages, Profile, **more...**
XMSR	XM SATELLITE	1:47pm 2.82	+0.52	+22.61%	3,109,444	Chart, Messages, Profile, **more...**
DISK	IMAGE ENTER	1:42pm 2.07	+0.32	+18.29%	55,900	Chart, Messages, Profile, **more...**
IEIB	INTL ELTR	10:15am 4.18	+0.61	+17.05%	2,000	Chart, Messages, Profile, **more...**
ATRI	ATRION CORP	12:58pm 23.50	+3.42	+17.03%	3,300	Chart, Messages, Profile, **more...**
DTAGY	DIGITALE TELE	9:41am 5.60	+0.81	+16.89%	500	Chart, Messages, Profile, **more...**
FIMG	FISCHER IMAGE	1:36pm 5.99	+0.84	+16.31%	109,500	Chart, Messages, Profile, **more...**
AVGN	AVIGEN INC	1:42pm 9.089	+1.169	+15.05%	184,243	Chart, Messages, Profile, **more...**
SCOR	SYNCOR INTL	1:47pm 29.79	+3.67	+14.05%	3,615,641	Chart, Messages, Profile, **more...**
OSTE	OSTEOTECH INC	1:44pm 6.27	+0.77	+14.00%	88,613	Chart, Messages, Profile, **more...**
FFEX	FROZEN FOOD EXP	1:41pm 2.55	+0.31	+13.84%	9,400	Chart, Messages, Profile, **more...**
NVDDC	NAVIDEC INC	1:34pm 2.25	+0.27	+13.64%	3,900	N/A
FPIC	FPIC INSURANCE	1:45pm 7.285	+0.874	+13.63%	156,400	Chart, Messages, Profile, **more...**
AHPI	ALLIED HLTHCARE	12:01pm 3.50	+0.40	+12.87%	1,100	Chart, Messages, Profile, **more...**
PLUM	PLUMTREE SFTWR	1:47pm 2.97	+0.33	+12.50%	485,728	Chart, Messages, Profile, **more...**
TPTI	TIPPINGPOINT	1:39pm 9.64	+1.03	+12.03%	4,800	Chart, Messages, Profile, **more...**
IFOX	INFOCROSSING	1:23pm 6.75	+0.69	+11.39%	12,400	Chart, Messages, Profile, **more...**
BJCT	BIOJECT MEDICL	1:31pm 2.39	+0.24	+11.16%	26,000	Chart, Messages, Profile, **more...**
FTUS	FACTORY 2U STRS	1:46pm 4.29	+0.40	+10.28%	468,826	Chart, Messages, Profile, **more...**
ENDOE	ENDOCARE INC	1:47pm 3.53	+0.31	+9.63%	755,600	Chart, Messages, Profile, **more...**
OLGR	OILGEAR CO	10:15am 2.77	0.00	0.00%	800	Chart, Messages, Profile, **more...**
PRAN	PRANA BIOTECH	1:42pm 9.50	+0.85	+9.83%	600	Messages, **more...**

Graph 4.5 Most Actives by Price Percentage Gain

In addition to retrieving the most active stocks by price or volume, you can also sort by which stocks show the highest or lowest percentage change for the day. For example, many investors focus on the stocks that have declined in percentage points, as those stocks may also have the most upside potential. Chart 4.6 illustrates the results of a search for "price percentage losers."

Symbol	Name	Last Trade		Change		Volume	Related Information
Volume Leaders: NASDAQ	AMEX	NYSE							
Price % Gainers: NASDAQ	AMEX	NYSE							
Price % Losers: NASDAQ	AMEX	NYSE					International: Europe	
XMSR	XM SATELLITE	3:42pm	2.21	-0.84	-27.54%	6,888,324	Chart, Msgs, Profile, more...
MILT	MILTOPE GROUP	3:42pm	3.42	-1.08	-24.00%	102,600	Chart, Msgs, Profile, more...
DYTKP	DYNTEK INC	3:40pm	2.34	-0.66	-22.00%	4,700	more...
FIMGE	FISCHER IMAGE	3:11pm	4.92	-1.05	-17.59%	25,400	Chart, Msgs, Profile, more...
DWMA	DICKIE WALKER	3:31pm	2.57	-0.43	-14.33%	5,600	Msgs, Profile, more...
NEON	NEON SYSTEMS	2:17pm	2.24	-0.341	-13.21%	1,400	Chart, Msgs, Profile, more...
BINX	BIONX IMPLANTS	10:34am	2.04	-0.31	-13.19%	100	Chart, Msgs, Profile, more...
AETC	APPLIED EXTRU	2:24pm	2.31	-0.35	-13.16%	18,800	Chart, Msgs, Profile, more...
RCCC	RURAL CELL A	3:40pm	2.01	-0.29	-12.61%	104,980	Chart, Msgs, Profile, more...
CTEC	CHOLESTECH CP	3:42pm	6.41	-0.85	-11.71%	77,193	Chart, Msgs, Profile, more...
RURL	RURAL/METRO	3:35pm	2.60	-0.35	-11.86%	211,800	Chart, Msgs, Profile, more...
HICKA	HICKOK CL A	3:05pm	4.25	-0.55	-11.46%	2,100	Chart, Msgs, Profile, more...
WATFZ	WATERFORD UN	1:12pm	4.00	-0.50	-11.11%	800	Chart, Msgs, Profile, more...
TAXI	MEDALLION FIN	3:42pm	4.10	-0.51	-11.06%	210,540	Chart, Msgs, Profile, more...
TBWC	TB WOODS CORP	3:02pm	5.88	-0.67	-10.23%	3,300	Chart, Msgs, Profile, more...
PARL	PARLUX FRAG	2:59pm	2.38	-0.269	-10.15%	41,500	Chart, Msgs, Profile, more...
WTRS	WATERS INSTR	10:25am	4.46	-0.50	-10.08%	1,300	Chart, Msgs, Profile, more...
MHCO	MOORE HANDLEY	9:30am	2.25	-0.25	-10.00%	200	Chart, Msgs, Profile, more...
SMHG	SANDERS MORRIS	2:20pm	6.95	-0.75	-9.74%	36,956	Chart, Msgs, Profile, more...
SRTI	SUNRISE TELECOM	3:26pm	2.14	-0.22	-9.32%	30,430	Chart, Msgs, Profile, more...
CLHB	CLEAN HARBORS	3:41pm	7.90	-0.80	-9.20%	212,458	Chart, Msgs, Profile, more...
CYTC	CYTYC CORP	3:42pm	9.87	-1.01	-9.28%	10,212,600	Chart, Msgs, Profile, more...
AMPL	AMPAL-AM ISRAEL	3:08pm	2.61	-0.26	-9.06%	29,700	Chart, Msgs, Profile, more...
SUPC	SUPERIOR CONSUL	3:41pm	2.05	-0.20	-8.89%	5,400	Chart, Msgs, Profile, more...

Chart 4.6 Most Actives by Price Percentage Loss

Charting Tools

Charts are fundamental decision-making tools when it comes to determining trend and momentum for stocks. Simple five-day charts like the one below are typically adequate for most traders, and are often included with your quote package through services such as Yahoo! Finance, or are available at no charge through your online brokerage firm. You should also subscribe to real-time charts, which are updated on a second-by-second basis throughout the day. Please refer to the "Real-Time Quotes" section earlier in this chapter for more information.

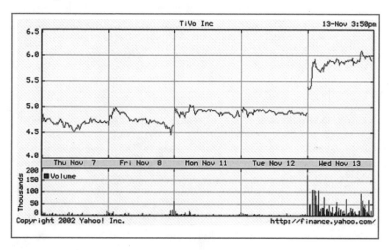

Chart 4.7 Five-day chart for TiVo

Charts can tell you a great deal about where a stock is headed. For example, in chart 4.7, you can see that TiVo (a manufacturer of digital video recorders) traded, for the most part, at relatively unchanged price and volume over a six-day period. You can also see this was followed by a sharp increase in both price and volume. Notice that on Wednesday, November 13, the stock opened and went up dramatically higher, then dropped moderately for a short period before going back up again. This type of drop typically signals the activity of professional investors who predicted the strong opening price and purchased the stock at the market opening or the day before. After the price rose, they took their profits and sold the stock, thereby driving the price down for a short period of time. This type of scenario provides an excellent buying opportunity for investors and is known as Buying on a Dip. (See chapter 7 for more information about this topic.)

While there are more advanced types of charts available through various software packages (such as Bollinger Bands and MACD), unless you become a near-professional investor or develop an interest in advanced technical analysis, the simple five-day and real-time intra-day charts will serve you well.

News Sources

CNBC

One of my favorite sources for news and information is the CNBC network. CNBC is a unique television channel in that it covers all aspects of investing, from stocks to bonds, and from money markets to commodities. It's always entertaining and up-to-date with what's going on in the markets, and has an incredible news team.

You'll find the special segments related to the current day's events particularly interesting. For example, in 2003, when a widespread blackout hit New York City, CNBC produced and aired a segment covering alternative power sources just hours after the lights went out. The coverage on both the blackout and its effects on the stock market were extensive and indispensable in allowing me to gauge how and when to trade.

The screens on CNBC also are convenient from a practical perspective. Real-time quotes of large block trades of more than 10,000 shares are conveniently displayed at the bottom of the screen. Watching these large block trades scroll across the screen during pre-trading hours really gives you a flavor of things to come during regular market hours. If someone is selling large blocks of IBM, for example, you might hypothesize that IBM will be coming out with negative earnings, bad news, or that some other event will be announced.

CNBC also has extensive coverage of geopolitical events through its parent company NBC, along with commentary and analyses to give you an idea of how international events and foreign markets will affect your investments.

With the *Lunchtime Millionaire* strategy, your primary focus will be on short-term news that causes short-term movements in the price of individual stocks. The news you'll want to pay attention to also will be of a relatively short-term nature. CNBC is perfect for uncovering information that will affect a company's stock price *today*.

I do recommend, however, also following a variety of other news sources to keep abreast of national and international events and to maintain a solid understanding of the financial markets in general. The following publications and news sources are particularly helpful. Most of these also offer free online access to their magazine for subscribers.

Dow Jones News

Dow Jones News is typically included with even the most basic financial packages available through sources such as Yahoo! Finance and brokerage houses.

Yahoo! Finance's news feed is actually a compilation of a number of news sources, including Reuters, Associated Press, SmartMoney, Forbes, and CBS Marketwatch. While the individual stories are not terribly comprehensive, you will be able to retrieve basic financial news such as earnings announcements, press releases, and national and international market information, throughout the day.

Silicon Valley Biz Ink (www.svbizink.com)

This newspaper focuses on four areas of coverage: technology, finance, real estate, and lifestyles, with an emphasis on technology. Biz Ink reports on "big picture" issues and the impact of technology on these areas.

Red Herring (www.redherring.com)

Red Herring covers innovation, technology, financing, and entrepreneurial activity. Its staff of award-winning journalists tells readers what's first, what matters, and most importantly, why it matters.

The San Jose Mercury News (www.mercnews.com)

Best known as the newspaper of record in Silicon Valley, the unofficial technology capital of the world.

The Wall Street Journal (www.wsj.com)

The world's leading business publication, covering virtually all aspects of financial news and information.

Investor's Business Daily (www.investors.com)

Considered more of a research tool than a traditional newspaper, this publication is known for its innovative stock tables, educational columns, and sophisticated professional-level analysis tools. It provides fundamental and technical evaluations on virtually every stock on the NASDAQ, the AMEX, and the NYSE.

Barron's (www.barrons.com)

Barron's touts itself as the magazine that delivers "the news before the market knows." Barron's is unique in that it provides a "backward-glancing" recap of the previous week's news, along with insights into what will happen in the week to come. The magazine and its website provide a more sophisticated take on trading, companies, and the market, and focus on anticipating market events.

Forbes (www.forbes.com)

Forbes offers commentary, analysis, tools and real-time original reporting on business, technology, investing, and lifestyle. Both its magazine and website include comprehensive company profiles, interactive tools, calculators, and databases, including People Tracker and the annual Forbes Lists.

Money and Money.com

Money.com is one of the Internet's leading sources for breaking business news, personal finance commentary, and planning tools. Working with the editors of Money magazine and the CNNfn television network, CNN/Money delivers all the day's pressing financial stories and goes beyond the headlines to show how they affect users' financial well-being.

TheStreet.com (www.thestreet.com)

A website started by Jim Cramer, a major contributor to CNBC. TheStreet.com's RealMoney is the one site for which I am willing to pay the $25 subscription fee. The information is comprehensive, insightful, fair, and balanced. I've found his in-depth analysis on various industries and stocks extremely helpful. In terms of recommending courses of action, The Street.com goes beyond the norm.

Yahoo! Finance (finance.yahoo.com)

This is a site I visit frequently and is one I consider among the best finance websites today. As you saw earlier in this chapter, it is priced reasonably and has everything: news, charts, "most actives" lists, downgrades and upgrades, company reports, message boards, and many other useful features.

Bloomberg.com (www.bloomberg.com)

Also a very helpful site, Bloomberg is a well-known and respected news source used by many professionals. Known for its accuracy and its detailed quote pages (with charts and fundamental data displayed together), Bloomberg covers the entire spectrum of stocks, from NYSE stocks to stocks listed on the Pink Sheets.

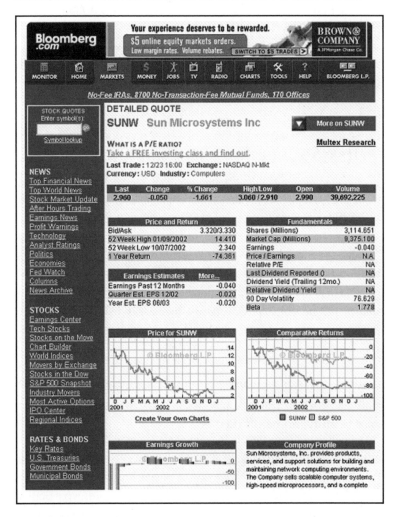

Chart 4.8 Quote Page from Bloomberg.com

In addition to its website, Bloomberg also has a broadcast news station that you can access over the Internet. A word of caution:

Bloomberg Television is best accessed via a Wi-Fi or a DSL connection, as its heavy video content requires a connection that can support it.

In order to view television-style financial programs such as Bloomberg on your computer, you will need Microsoft's Windows Media Player or RealNetworks' Real One player, both of which can be downloaded for free.

OTHER SOURCES OF INFORMATION

Message Boards

Message boards are online forums for individual investors to share information and ideas on the stock market and specific companies. Message boards are particularly helpful if you wish to learn about smaller public companies, because networks like CNBC rarely cover them.

Generally speaking, the larger news sources follow only a few hundred stocks or so at any given time. There are a great number of small companies with tremendous potential, so it always makes sense to hunt around for them.

While helpful in gauging investor sentiment, message boards can be somewhat controversial because of what's known as "pump and dump." It is not uncommon for an investor who holds a particular stock to sometimes post misleading comments about the company in hopes of driving up the price (pumping). Once the stock price reaches a certain level, he or she "dumps" the stock and sells it at a profit. If the "pumper" holds a large position of a relatively infrequently traded stock, the price can drop dramatically, leaving the rest of the investors with a loss on their hands.

Pumping and dumping is highly unethical. If you suspect that someone on a message board is engaging in the practice, proceed with caution. Some novice investors are tempted to buy early in the pump game, riding on the coattails of the pumper, but this is never a good idea. The stock may become so volatile that you'll find yourself getting dumped along with everyone else.

The bottom line is, when checking the news and rumors on message boards, take what you read with a grain of salt, and always check other sources of information before placing a trade.

If you are interested in learning more about the practice of pumping and dumping, I encourage you to visit the official SEC page, www.sec.gov/answers/pumpdump.htm, which covers the practice at length.

There are currently three primary message boards that you'll find helpful in researching news and rumors on stocks. All three boost a high level of participation among the investment community.

Raging Bull www.ragingbull.com

Silicon Investor www.siliconinvestor.com

Yahoo! Finance finance.Yahoo.com

To participate in a message board, visit the site and follow the instructions for setting up an account. If you already have an account with Yahoo! Finance, for example, you can simply visit the finance page, click on Community, then Boards, or enter a stock symbol, then click on the Message Board link. There you can read what people have to say about the stocks in which you are interested. You'll also find instructions on each message board on how to post your own comments.

Messages boards aren't always for the faint of heart. While on some message boards, such as Silicon Investor, discussions are conducted politely and professionally, on others, you may hear a great deal of swearing and hyperbole.

Useful Websites

Island/INET (www.isld.com)

Besides being one the most prominent ECNs (Electronic Communication Networks), Island also offers very useful and efficient "most actives" lists of stocks, not only during the official hours of trading but, most importantly, before the opening and after the closing of the markets. If you're looking for pre- or post-market action, Island, with its easy-to-access "Top 20" list, is the place to visit.

data.island.com - Microsoft Internet Explorer

Island Top List | back | refresh | www.island.com | data.island.com | help
All Stocks ETFs Listed Stocks

Top 5 Top 20 Top 50 Top 100 | Regular Hours After Hours

#	Symbol	MKT	Shares Matched	Last Price	Last Match Time	Open Orders	Net Change	Percent Change
1	SUNW	NM	1,938,897	3.3080	19:58:47.4	0	+0.3400	+11.46
2	QQQ	AM	259,071	25.6490	19:35:55.3	0	-0.0210	-0.08
3	CSCO	NM	89,987	13.4700	19:57:39.7	0	+0.0300	+0.22
4	INTC	NM	73,352	17.1800	19:59:25.6	0	-0.0300	-0.17
5	RDRT	NM	70,800	0.3300	19:40:56.6	0	+0.0010	+0.30
6	ITWO	NM	70,271	1.1600	19:46:02.7	0	+0.0200	+1.75
7	MSFT	NM	65,517	53.9300	19:58:57.1	0	-0.0700	-0.13
8	JDSU	NM	62,960	2.5700	18:13:38.4	0	+0.0100	+0.39
9	RFMD	NM	62,693	7.3000	19:58:41.1	0	+0.0200	+0.27
10	NXTL	NM	59,617	13.2500	19:46:44.7	0	+0.0600	+0.45
11	ADSX	SC	55,552	0.4300	19:39:37.2	0	-0.0200	-4.44
12	ORCL	NM	41,851	11.0110	19:42:46.4	0	-0.0490	-0.44
13	XMSR	NM	40,715	3.0700	18:18:28.5	0	-0.1200	-3.76
14	SPY	AM	39,902	89.9500	18:31:28.3	0	-0.0700	-0.08
15	BRCD	NM	37,502	4.4900	18:16:40.7	0	-0.0100	-0.22
16	CIEN	NM	37,246	5.7500	19:51:48.7	0	+0.0400	+0.70
17	INKT	NM	36,927	1.5900	18:22:24.8	0	-0.0100	-0.62
18	AMAT	NM	36,197	13.9100	19:50:07.1	0	-0.0300	-0.22
19	RBAK	NM	32,906	0.7500	19:38:01.2	0	-0.0100	-1.32
20	SEBL	NM	32,846	7.9800	19:53:52.5	0	+0.1300	+1.66

As of 20:00:29.73 Terms of Use

Chart 4.9 - Island's Top-20 List

Ameritrade (www.ameritrade.com)

If you have an account with the discount brokerage firm Ameritrade, you have free access to one of best financial packages available, the Ameritrade Streamer. Ameritrade's service features streaming quotes with a nicely connected order entry system with which you can place a buy or sell order simply by clicking on the appropriate streaming quote button. You are then forwarded to the order entry page, where all the parameters have been entered. Once you press the confirm key, your order is placed.

Chart 4.10 shows a sample of one of the most popular Ameritrade stock monitoring screens. Bid price, ask price, and volume can be monitored in real time. Bid and ask prices are highlighted in green or red depending on the direction of the price change.

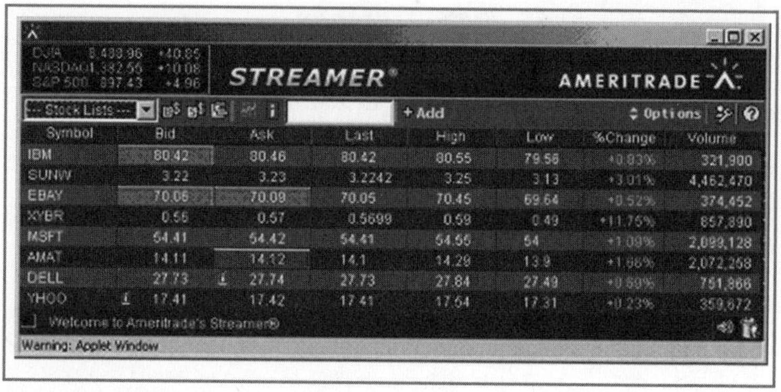

Chart 4.10 Ameritrade Streamer.

E*Trade (www.etrade.com)

Investors who open an account with E*Trade also have a number of powerful tools available to them. The best of these, Power E*Trade, is available to frequent traders who qualify. Power E*Trade includes a tool called Market Trader, with which you can retrieve one of the greatest concentrations of real-time information on the Web. From real-time level II quotes to real-time news, Market Trader has it all. You can even place trades without having to leave the Market Trader screen. See Chart 4.11.

To qualify for Power E*Trade, you are required to (as of this writing) be an "active trader." This means that you have to have placed at least 27 trades during the last quarter. With the *Lunchtime*

Millionaire strategy, this level is not difficult to achieve if you buy and sell stocks every day, or even every other day.

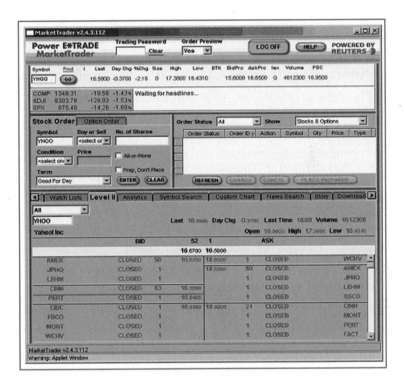

Chart 4.11 E*Trade's Market Trader Screen

Townsend Analytics (www.Townsend.com)

Townsend Analytics offers software called "RealTick," which is a professional-level tool available to individual investors at a fairly affordable price. With RealTick, you can create an unlimited number of fully customizable pages, which you will use to monitor hundreds of stocks in real time.

Because you are setting the parameters of what you'll see, the RealTick windows can be designed either to show complete information on all financial instruments, or just a recap. You can resize data windows, set chart parameters, change font size, and choose your color preferences.

My favorite RealTick feature is the ability to dynamically sort any of the columns you choose to display. For example, you can sort the information displayed by: price percentage increase for the day, ask price, total volume, or any number of other factors. Sorting by price percentage change allows you to determine which stocks are up at any given time, and by how much. This tells you where the action is in real-time.

Townsend Analytics' technology is so efficient that you can monitor thousands of stocks simultaneously—potentially the entire 10,000 plus stocks in the stock market, if you so desire. If you happen to have fast computer and Internet connections, RealTick will allow you to view every trade placed by any market participant in the world.

Now that you've become familiar with the various tools offered by different providers, how do you choose which ones are right for you? Visit each of the websites I've mentioned, and spend some time poking around. While some features will be impossible to explore fully without opening an account, many companies allow you to open trial accounts without making a long-term commitment.

CHAPTER FIVE

Where to Trade

Trading on your lunch hour has many advantages, the primary one being the ability to trade virtually anywhere. You can set up shop in locations as diverse as coffee shops, restaurants, airline terminals, hotel lobbies, even fast food restaurants like McDonald's. I've even been known to open my laptop in parks, waiting rooms, and the front seat of my car.

Because trading locations can range from poor to ideal, in the following pages I've outlined the most important factors to consider. When discussing wireless providers and plans, I've tried to be as specific as possible.

Technology changes rapidly, however, so please feel free to visit my website, www.lunchtimemillionaire.com, for up-to-date information.

CHOOSING A WIRELESS PLAN

For those of you who are planning to subscribe to wireless Internet access, you'll find that your trading locations will be limited only by the availability of wireless service. You'll have two methods of receiving wireless capabilities on your laptop: 1) via a Wi-Fi connection provided by the restaurant, coffee shop or other venue, or 2) via your own 3G wireless connection. As I mentioned in chapter 2, regardless of which method you use, your laptop computer will need to be wireless-enabled with either a PCMCIA card or built-in wireless technology.

When first subscribing to a wireless service, you will be provided with an ID and password to access your wireless provider's network, a method similar to the way you access the Internet from your home computer. Each time you sign on to the wireless network, a kind of "hand-shake" will take place between your computer and the service provider's transmitters.

The usage fees for the time you spend online will most likely be included in the monthly fee you pay to your wireless provider, as long as you stay within a specific geographic area. When traveling outside that area, you will normally incur roaming charges for the time you spend online. If you travel regularly, and want to avoid these additional charges, you'll need to sign up for a national wireless plan, similar to the way you might choose a national plan with your cell phone provider.

Wherever you are, you will want to test the quality of the wireless signal before you start your trading session. The last thing you want is a lost connection right as you are poised to hit the send button. As you go along, you'll start to get a good sense of where in your chosen trading "neighborhood" you have a consistently reliable connection, and where you don't.

CONNECTIONS PROVIDED BY VENUES

In this age of the Internet, more and more restaurants and coffee shops are making wireless Internet access available to their customers via Wi-Fi. To take advantage of a venue's Internet service, you'll need to subscribe to the same wireless service provider to which it subscribes.

For instance, Starbucks Coffee shops nationwide make T-Mobile wireless service available to their customers. If you'd like to access the Internet using Starbucks' provider, your computer will need to be T-Mobile enabled as well. Another coffee shop down the street may offer Deep Blue Wireless to its customers, in which case you'll want to be enabled for Deep Blue when trading at that site.

USING YOUR OWN INTERNET CONNECTION

The alternative to using a location's wireless service is to use your own 3G technology. 3G is a technology that allows you to trade virtually anywhere, regardless of the service provided by the venue in which you are presently located. Since 3G service utilizes some of the same technology as your cell phone service, a rule of thumb is that wherever you can receive wireless phone service, you'll be able to receive 3G service. As of this writing, 3G service is provided by a number of providers, including Verizon and Sprint.

Wi-Fi connections are typically faster than 3G, hence you'll likely want to take advantage of the service provided by the venue. As of this writing, however, Verizon is rolling out a faster version of 3G, which should improve response time. In order to have the widest range of location choices, I currently subscribe to T-Mobile Wi-

Fi and Verizon 3G. This way, I have coverage nearly everywhere I go.

TRADING IN A RESTAURANT

Restaurants are usually willing to allow you to work on your laptop computer at your table or at the bar. It's normally not even necessary to ask permission. When trading in a restaurant, I often choose one with a bar that serves food in addition to drinks because I like the ability to spread out. Whenever possible, I also try to sit at the end of the bar where there is a bit more privacy. If I'm using my 3G wireless connection, I sit near a window where the signal is typically stronger. (If I'm using the venue's Internet connection, the speed will be the same no matter where I sit.)

How can you determine whether a particular restaurant offers Internet access? Just call ahead. The person answering the phone should be familiar with the type of Internet access the restaurant makes available to its customers. If the restaurant does not offer wireless, I suggest you drop a note to its management requesting that it does.

As you begin to trade on your lunch hour, you may want to patronize moderately priced restaurants. Your trading levels, and hence profits, will be moderate initially, and it will be discouraging if you come away at the end of the first week having spent more on lunch than you've made on your investments. While many people prefer to patronize quiet, secluded restaurants, I've found that I enjoy restaurants that tend to be noisy. That might seem counterintuitive, but sometimes background noise allows me to disconnect from my surroundings and concentrate better on the financial markets.

When trading in a restaurant, be careful what you order. I've heard more horror stories about spilled soup on laptop computers than I care to recount. Try to order food with the least potential for spilling, and be particularly careful with condiments like mustard and mayonnaise.

A final note about trading in a restaurant: Be sure to pick a venue that is safe. Laptops are popular items to steal, so even if the bartender or waiter promises to watch your computer while you're in the restroom, don't let it leave your side.

TRADING FROM A COFFEE SHOP

Over the last decade, coffee shops have become the location of choice for writers, professionals, and students in search of an inspiring and fairly quiet place in which to work. Many coffee shops offer sandwiches, cookies, and other snacks, which makes lunchtime trading convenient. Space can be a bit of a problem, but if you plan ahead, you can usually arrive before the other patrons and secure a table. The number of coffee shops that offer wireless Wi-Fi service is growing dramatically, so access to trading is fairly easy to find. Please visit my website, www.lunchtimemillionaire. com, for a nationwide guide to wireless-enabled coffee shops.

TRADING WHILE TRAVELING

If you would like to trade while traveling, you may want to subscribe to a nationwide plan. Doing so will enable you to take advantage of Internet services on the road without coming home to an outrageously high wireless bill at the end of the month.

Hotels

Many hotels now offer their guests a number of methods for connecting to the Internet, including dial–up, DSL, and/or Wi-Fi service. The Four Seasons and Marriott hotels both offer wireless service at this time, and I expect that other chains are not far behind. Often these connections are provided in the guest rooms as well as the business services area of the hotel.

If you've signed up for 3G service and happen to be in an area where your 3G service is not available, you'll likely be able to access the Internet via the hotel's own offerings. Of course, if you'd like to use the hotel's Internet connection, your computer will need to be configured appropriately with either dial-up, DSL, or Wi-Fi software and service capability.

For example, if you use the hotel's dial-up capability, you'll need an account with an Internet provider. For DSL, you'll need an Ethernet card (often available at hotels), and for Wi-Fi, you'll need to have in your laptop the required PC card or built-in wireless capability and a subscription to a Wi-Fi service. Wi-Fi capabilities, however, will typically only be accessible in public areas like the lobby.

Planes and Airports

It is 12:15 p.m. Pacific time, the stock market is closing in 45 minutes, and you're inside the airport. At the time of this writing, many major U.S. airports and airline club rooms are Wi-Fi enabled, so you can check the markets and even place a trade. In smaller airports, you may have to use a 3G connection instead. Some airlines are already offering Internet access Internet on flights.

TRADING AT THE OFFICE

Although it's always tempting to trade at work, there are a number of problems inherent in doing so. While the Internet connection might be extremely reliable and lightning fast, you can be assured that at least once during a critical trading point, your manager or a colleague will interrupt you with an important question. Most managers won't look favorably on the employee who responds to a request with, "I'm in the midst of a trade and can't talk right now."

In addition to the interruptions that will inevitably happen while trading at work, it is likely that your company will have a policy stipulating that employees not use the company computers or Internet connection for personal use.

In reality, most companies tolerate the use of the computer for personal use when it is very limited. But as personal e-mail and the Internet become more common, many companies are finding that employee abuse is rampant. If word gets out that you are trading on company property using a company computer and Internet access, you can pretty much bet you'll be asked to stop.

Besides, I'm a firm believer in the benefits of midday breaks to get away from the office and have some time to yourself. Breaking away for an hour allows you to switch your mind to your hobby, forget about the office for a while, and completely focus on research, trading and, of course, eating.

Trading from a Park

This is the life, isn't it? Making money and relaxing outdoors at the same time. I sometimes trade in a park and enjoy it very much. While this means you have to use the slower 3G wireless connection, it works faster outdoors.

I recommend selecting a location that is relatively private and that discourages passers-by from asking questions about your computer and what you're doing with it. Putting people off is never easy, particularly when you're in the midst of placing a trade.

Once again, watch out for thieves. Even in the nicest parks in the safest areas, never leave your laptop unguarded.

Trading from Home

If your home is the most convenient place for you to trade, chances are you'll be using a desktop computer rather than your laptop. Whichever type of computer you use, I recommend that you reserve it for your private use. If you allow children and other family members to use the same computer you use for trading, you may wake up one morning to find that the computer no longer boots or that your files have been corrupted.

CHAPTER SIX

Strategy Number 1: The Last Hour of Trading

The Last Hour of Trading strategy is based on the belief held by many professional investors that the final hour of market trading is the optimal hour to trade. As I will explain further, professionals use this time to buy stocks that show momentum during the final hour and sell them at a profit as early as the opening or pre-opening hours of the market the following day. The Last Hour of Trading conveniently corresponds with lunch time in the Western United States.

I fell into this new trading strategy somewhat accidentally. Because I lived on the West Coast, I often began my trading day before going to work in the morning. I'd follow the market for half an hour or so, then head off to work and take another break at noon to finish my trading for the day. Since my morning ritual happened to coincide with the market opening on the East Coast, and my lunch hour coincided with the last hour of market trading, I traded my portfolio on this schedule for quite some time. Over time, I began to notice patterns and trends in the way the market and individual stocks responded in relationship to those two time periods of the day. I began to realize that the two most important moments in a trading day are the opening and the closing of the markets.

I noticed that, frequently, stocks that showed an upward trend at the end of the day opened even higher the next morning. For that reason, buying stocks before the markets closed while having lunch, and selling at the opening of the markets in the morning before I went to work the next day, became one of my favorite trading strategies.

What causes the increase in stock prices between the close of market one day and the open in the market the next? After the close of market, institutional investors continue to work, talk, research, and share information. By the time they arrive at work the following morning before the market opens, they often already know which trades they intend to make. When the markets open, these institutional investors place opening bids, pushing prices up, before the little guys even get around to calling their brokers.

If you live in a time zone other than the Pacific, the Last Hour of Trading won't necessarily coincide with your lunch hour. You can still, however, take advantage of the momentum trading techniques described here. With the advent of home offices, flex time, and extended market hours, even Midwest and East Coast investors can use the Last Hour of Trading strategy. Many employees, for example, have a flexible enough schedule to take a short break at noon Eastern Time to research their investments, an extended coffee break at 3 P.M. EST to place their buy orders, and time before work during pre-opening market hours from 8 to 9:30 A.M. EST to place their sell orders.

For example, if you live in Denver, you might go to lunch at 1 P.M. In Chicago, you could take a late lunch at 2 P.M. Many of my clients find this an ideal time to trade, as cafés and restaurants are much less crowded following the main lunch rush. For folks on the East Coast, 3 p.m. may be a great time to take an extended coffee break.

Table 6.2 shows the timing of investment activities for the six U.S. time zones. Before we delve into the time zones in detail, however, it's useful to understand why the final hour of the trading session is so advantageous. First, the various stock-related news alerts, press releases, and economic data disseminated throughout the day are likely to have moved the markets in one direction or another. During the Last Hour of Trading, however, the markets frequently move sharply, either in the opposite, or the same, direction as they've been moving throughout the day. This can occur for a number of reasons:

- **Overestimating negative news**: Sometimes institutional investors who have been anticipating negative market news and have sold their positions discover during the final market hour that that the news is not as negative as they anticipated. They rush to repurchase the stock, driving the price up.

- **Profit taking:** The market has been up for the day and institutional investors decide to sell their positions in order to lock in their profits. This can cause a sharp decrease in the price of individual stocks, bringing down the market as a whole.

These sharp, end-of-market up-and-down trends often indicate where the markets will head the following day of trading. Your main concern with the Last Hour of Trading strategy, however, will not be the direction of the market as a whole, but rather the movement, or momentum, of individual stocks. Your goal is to pick a potential winner, a stock that is showing a temporary up trend, so that you can buy during its upward trend and sell before it starts a downward trend. In doing so, your goal will be to realize a profit in the neighborhood of 3 to 7 percent in a very short period of time, typically within 24 to 48 hours.

Implementing Your Strategy

The Last Hour of Trading strategy is simple to implement, and no matter what time zone you live in, can be made to fit your workday. You won't necessarily trade every day. In fact, most *Lunchtime Millionaire* investors will make trades only a few times each week. To demonstrate how to put your strategy to work on the days you do trade, I've detailed below a typical daily schedule, along with the price and volume indicators to watch for. I've used Pacific Coast Time in my description, so if you trade on Mountain, Central, or Eastern Time, you'll want to adjust the schedule accordingly.

- 6 A.M. PST: Wake up, eat breakfast and turn on CNBC to get a feel for where the markets are headed. Remember that whether the markets are expected to open higher or lower should not substantially influence your trading strategy. However, you should still stay abreast of major news events.

- 6:15 A.M. PST: Log on to your computer, the Internet, and your brokerage house screen. Open real-time quotes and real-time charts. Briefly check the latest financial news to get a sense of what's going on with the markets as a whole. Check your watch list for news and activity on the stocks you hold.

- 6:30 A.M. PST: The markets open. If the stocks you purchased the day before show a rise of 3 percent or more, it's time to sell. Remember, the goal is to make many small profits, not single large ones.

- 6:45 A.M. PST: Begin your search for stocks to purchase today. Retrieve a list of the top ten NASDAQ stocks that are most active for the day. Begin to research a few of them. Make a list of stocks that may have buy potential, along with a few brief notes on potential buy and sell prices.

- 7 A.M. PST: Take a shower and get ready to go to work.

- 8 or 9 A.M. PST: Arrive at the office.

- 12 noon PST: Take your laptop and head out for lunch at your favorite restaurant or cafe.

- 12:10 P.M. PST: Power on your computer, then log on to the Internet and your brokerage house screen. Open real-time quotes and real-time charts. Briefly check the latest financial news. Check the top ten most actives again and recheck the research you conducted in the morning.

- 12:25 P.M. PST: You start noticing a few stocks that show good upside momentum. One company, in particular, released news at the beginning of the day, a partnership with a FORTUNE 100 company. The stock is up 20 percent already (from $3 to $3.60). You open up a window to watch each individual trade that is placed for the stock, whether a buy order or a sell order. This window is called a level II ticker.

- 12:35 P.M. PST: The stock you have been monitoring for 10 minutes is now going through a pullback (a significant price increase followed by a price drop). This typically occurs at the end of the day when investors often decide to lock in their profit. Because sellers outnumber buyers, at least for a short while, the price goes down. At this moment, the sellers are now asking for $3.40 a share (the ask price).

- 12:45 P.M. PST: The pullback is over. The stock price is going back up. The ask price is now $3.70, and it's time to buy. You quickly bring up your calculator to see how many shares you can buy given the current stock price and funds you have on deposit at your brokerage house. You place a limit buy order at $3.80 (a limit order will guarantee that you don't pay more than a certain price for the stock). You take a few moments to think about your goals for the following trading day, and consider the prices at which you'll want to sell should the stock price go up or down.

- 12:55 P.M. PST: The markets are about to close as you're finishing your lunch. Your stock has gone back to the $4 level. It's time to head back to the office.

Another advantage in waiting until the end of the day to trade is that you can refer to intra-day charts to help you predict whether stocks that were up during the day will continue their upward trend. For example, let's take a look at the activity of Sina Corporation (SINA), an online media company based in China, at the end of the trading day of December 20, 2002.

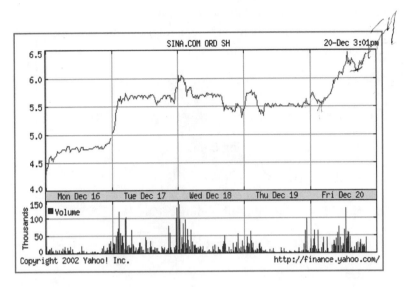

Chart 6.1

SINA went up from $5.50 to $6.50 in the middle of the day on no news. That's an 18 percent increase. The move to $6.50 was then followed by a pullback and a subsequent upward movement. That's exactly the kind of move to look for—a stock that rises, falls a bit, then rises again at the end of the trading day. That is the definition of an upward trend that has legs. Chances are good that the stock will open at a higher price the following day which, incidentally, it did.

Taking Advantage of Your Time Zone

Table 6.3 shows how trading hours vary depending upon where in the country you live.

The market hours called regular session are the hours between the first ringing of the bell (the one in the morning) and the second ringing of the bell (the one in the afternoon) at the New York Stock Exchange. Most of the trading activity takes place during the market hours. Investors also can buy and sell stocks outside market hours, either before the opening, or after the closing, of the regular session.

Table 6.2

East Coast

- 8 A.M.: Pre-opening hours

- 9:30 A.M.: Market opens

- 3 P.M.: Last hour of trading begins

- 4–8 P.M.: After-market hours trading

Central

- 7 A.M.: Pre-opening hours

- 8:30 A.M.: Market opens

- 2 P.M.: Last hour of trading begins

- 3–7 P.M.: After-market hours trading

Mountain

- 6 A.M.: Pre-opening hours

- 7:30 A.M.: Market opens

- 1 P.M.: Last hour of trading begins

- 2– 6 P.M.: After-market hours trading

Pacific Coast

- 5 A.M.: Pre-opening hours

- 6:30 A.M.: Market opens

- 12 P.M.: Last hour of trading begins

- 1–5 P.M.: After-market hours trading

Alaska

- 4 A.M.: Pre-opening hours

- 5:30 A.M.: Market opens

- 11 A.M.: Last hour of trading begins

- 12– 4 P.M.: After-market hours trading

Hawaii

- 3 A.M.: Pre-opening hours

- 4:30 A.M.: Market opens

- 10 A.M.: Last hour of trading begins

- 11–3 P.M.: After-market hours trading

While the final hour of trading strategy is a relatively simple one, it is one that has been extremely profitable for professional and non-professional investors alike. If you're lucky enough to live on the West Coast, it will coincide perfectly with your lunch hour. If you reside in the East or the Midwest, with a little creative scheduling you'll still find the strategy just as beneficial.

CHAPTER SEVEN

Strategy Number 2: Buying on a Dip

A s you saw earlier in the book, companies frequently wait until after the market closes before releasing news regarding their products and earnings. These after-market news releases often occur after the closing bell, or just before the market opens for pre-market trading between 8 and 9:30 A.M. EST.

Experienced investors watch carefully for these pre-opening and after-closing news releases. Following good news, you'll often see a steady increase in share price at the beginning of pre-market trading as a rush of investors jump to buy or sell stocks based on these reports. This rise will often then be followed by a sharp decrease in share price as investors sell and collect their profits, known as profit-taking. The stock price will most likely stop falling. This decrease followed by an increase creates a "dip."

Specifically, when the markets open again for regular trading hours, there will always be a number of investors who did not take advantage of pre-opening hours or after-hours trading the day before. When they turn on their computers in the morning and read the good news, they'll also jump on board, causing the stock price to go back up.

A little bit later, as the stock keeps going up, those who jumped on the stock right at the opening start considering an exit strategy. As the stock price reaches a level some believe will be the high for the day, profit-taking occurs once again. The stock then goes back down to a price level other investors will find attractive, causing the stock to go back up, completing a second dip.

Visually speaking, these two dips create an "M" pattern. Additional dips may occur later during the session.

Following is the series of events that occurs, hour by hour:

- 8 A.M. EST: Pre-opening market hours begin. Experienced investors react to either post-closing news from the day before or pre-opening news from the current day. If the news is positive, and investors start to place buy orders, the stock price will rise.

- 8:30–9:30 A.M. EST: Before regular trading hours even start, many experienced investors will sell their holdings to take a profit. In this type of circumstance, it is not unusual to see a dramatic decrease in share price, sometimes as much as 20 or 30 percent. This might be the time to jump in and place your buy order.

- 9:30 A.M. EST: The market opens. Investors who did not participate in pre-opening trading begin to read the news and place buy orders, driving up the share price once again (the first dip).

- 9:30–10 A.M. EST: Because of that sudden rise in price, a wave of profit-takers will then step in to sell their shares, causing the price to decrease again, likely followed by an increase (the second dip). However, if the outlook on the company is especially favorable, or if the company's positive news happens to be covered by the major television or radio networks, the stock, instead of seeing waves of profit-taking, will maintain a steady upward trajectory. During times such as these, the opportunity to take advantage of the dip strategy will decrease.

- 10 A.M.–3 P.M. EST: Market trading is typically slower during the middle of the day, and while you may see a number of dips, the opportunity for finding great deals will be diminished. Given that you will either be going to work or at work during this time period, you wouldn't be tracking your stocks during these hours anyway.

- 3–4 P.M. EST: The last hour of market trading is an optimal time to buy stocks because the direction a stock takes during that final hour often gives an indication of where the price will open the following morning. Chapter 6 covers the final hour of market trading.

This strategy, Buying on a Dip, is designed to take advantage of these ups and downs in price.

The chart 7.1 shows a real-life example of when dips occur.

In March 2003, Futuremedia PLC, a British software company, saw its stock price gradually rise over a four-day period. There was no immediate or dramatic news about the company. However, there had been several minor news stories during that time that had put a positive spin on the stock. Investors gradually increased their buys of the stock, pushing the price up. On March 30, the stock finished strong. The morning of March 31, during pre-opening hours, new investors began buying the stock, which drove the price even higher. Those investors then took their profits, causing the stock price to decrease just before the opening of regular market hours. As a savvy investor, you noticed how high the stock price went during pre-opening hours. You also noticed the sharp decrease before the opening of regular market hours. Having not seen any negative news that would have caused the decrease, you concluded it was caused by profit-taking. Anticipating the subsequent increase, you then bought the stock.

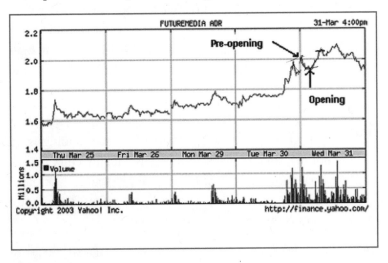

Chart 7.1

When Not to Use the Dip Strategy

When considering using the dip strategy, only buy a stock when you conclude that a lower price is the result of profit-taking. If the lower price is the result of bad news, it's difficult to determine how low the share price will go. Here is an example.

In August 2003, Dow Jones reported that Microsoft (MSFT) was re-evaluating its contract with a company called LookSmart (LOOK), an Internet search engine firm. Up until that time, LookSmart had performed extremely well. In fact, for the three months ending in March 2003, revenues rose 67 percent to $33.4 million. However, those revenues relied heavily on fees the company earned from providing the search functionality for Microsoft's MSN Internet service. Once the news of the re-evaluation hit, rumors began to fly that LookSmart might be in trouble. On Friday, August 15, LookSmart's price began to fall. Some investors believed at the time that, while the rumors were negative, the price of the stock would soon recover. However, on Monday, August 18, stock analysts following the company lowered their recommendations on the stock from "Buy" to "Hold," causing the share price to fall further.

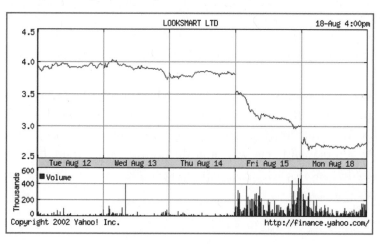

Chart 7.2

The case of LookSmart is not unusual. Bad news often snowballs. As sellers rush to get out, analysts who follow the stock begin to re-evaluate their recommendations.

So why not take advantage of a falling share price in the hopes of a recovery? Remember, the Buying on a Dip strategy works when there is good news or no news at all. It assumes that the primary reason the share price declined was that traders who had bought before the price rose are now taking their profits. Buying on a Dip also assumes that you will buy and sell a stock in a relatively short period of time. It's important to buy stocks that will recover from their decreases within that period of time. Share prices that fall on bad news may or may not recover in the short term. Rather than putting your attention on a stock that is declining on bad news, there are plenty of opportunities to take advantage of the price fluctuations of fundamentally sound stocks.

When Else Shouldn't You Participate in the Dip Strategy

Let's say you've turned on your computer and pulled up a chart depicting pre-opening trading for computer giant Dell. Instead of seeing a strong and defined upturn followed by a strong and defined downturn as profit takers sell, you see a series of many up-and-down movements. A series of small fluctuations may indicate that there is not a strong consensus about the news. When the sentiment wavers in this way, it's much more difficult to determine when, or if, to jump in. It's far less certain what the day will bring.

Choosing the Right Stocks for the Dip Strategy

How do you decide which stocks to buy? I have found that the dip strategy works best with NASDAQ stocks because they tend to have higher volatility than AMEX and NYSE stocks. This doesn't necessarily mean that the shares will always fluctuate widely, but it does mean that the percentage increase will be enough that if your trading strategy pans out, you can walk away with a profit in a relatively short period of time. In contrast, it's fairly rare to see an NYSE stock up 20 percent or more in any given trading day.

Before I talk further about how to choose the right dip stocks, it's worth mentioning a few words about market data providers. As I mentioned earlier in the book, it is essential that you subscribe to a service that provides real-time data. With the more volatile stocks, a delay of 15 minutes can make the difference between participating in a profitable rise and fall and sitting on the sidelines.

It is also important to subscribe to a service that follows real-time pre- and post-market trading, with both quotes and charts. Even if you never plan to get up early enough to trade during pre-market hours, you'll still want the ability to see what happened during that times. Two good service providers for after-market pricing and charts are Island and Archipelago. Many discount brokers, such as E*Trade, relay information from those two companies, so you don't necessarily have to sign up for their services. Check first with your brokerage to determine if you can receive the services for free.

Once you've set up your system with real-time quotes and pre- and post-market data, you can begin the search for your dip candidates. Following are the steps I recommend taking each morning when you begin your search.

STEP 1

Pull up a real-time list of NASDAQ top price percentage gainers. You can use a number of different service vendors, such as Yahoo! Finance, E*Trade, or Bloomberg for this information, just be sure the quotes are real-time. The price percentage gainers are those stocks that have had the largest percentage increase in price. These are the best dip candidates because their prices have had enough of an upward trend that investors will choose to sell and take their profits. This brings the price down, and so gives you the opportunity to buy at a lower price before the price goes back up.

The very fact that a company makes it to the top price percentage gainers list snowballs interest on The Street. As a matter of fact, when a company releases good news, institutional investors and stock analysts take note. That leads to increased media attention. When the media jumps in, individual investors hop on the bandwagon. Soon a winner becomes a mega-winner.

Of the 25 or so stocks in the list, look for and eliminate the "flukes." For instance, you see a stock that is thinly traded, with volume of less than 5,000 shares, yet the price is up 30 percent. When you investigate, you see the stock closed at $3.00 the day before, and opened the following day at $4.00. This is known as an unusual trading pattern. When a stock opens 30 percent higher than the price at which it closes, it usually indicates that there are not enough buyers and sellers making competing offers. It then becomes a seller's market—the seller can name his price, and the buyer has no alternative.

On the flip side, low volume stocks can also be tough for sellers to sell because there are fewer buyers. In this scenario, you'll often see wide variances in the bid and ask prices of the stock. Unfortunately, there are few SEC policies regulating the spread between the bid and ask prices, and investors often must wait things out or trade at undesirable levels.

STEP 2

After eliminating the flukes, choose ten of the top price percentage gainers from the remainder of the list. Focusing on high percentage gainers allows you to choose stocks that will be more likely to have the peaks and valleys you are looking for.

STEP 3

Next, narrow your selection to those stocks that also show decent volume, i.e., hundreds of thousands or even millions of shares exchanged within an hour or so (note: the volume displayed on the quotes and charts includes the pre-opening volume). Remember, high volume means people are interested in the stock, and you'll have many more opportunities to find a seller when you want to buy and a buyer when you want to sell.

Never focus on stocks that show high price increases without correspondingly reasonably high volume.

STEP 4

Once you've identified the stocks with the greatest percentage price increase and/or highest volume, retrieve a five-day chart for each stock on that list. Over time, I've noticed that the most successful strategy is to focus on stocks that show either 1) a steady, but not dramatic increase over the last few days, or 2) a flat pattern over the last few days, followed by a sudden increase in volume and price. This often indicates that something big is on the horizon.

Even when no news has been released, rumors are often bounding around The Street and anticipation is building.

STEP 5

After choosing your best percentage gainers and analyzing the five-day charts, the next step is to review the news. If you have an account at a brokerage firm such as E*Trade, which consolidates and makes available most, if not all, of the best news sources to its clients, you can easily navigate between your trading screen and the news. Otherwise, I recommend Yahoo! Finance or Bloomberg, which both carry very fast and up-to-the-minute news. All of these companies gather their reports from major news providers such as Dow Jones, Reuters, Financial Times, and Forbes.

When reviewing the news about your price percentage gainers, look for good news, such as companies with new management, new partnerships, stock splits, stock repurchase plans, insider buying, or restructuring. I often find that old high-flyers, such as Internet companies that are making comebacks, are ideal stocks to consider buying. Even layoffs sometimes indicate a new management's strategy to put the ship back on course.

Now, it's important to realize that when you click to a company's summary page, you will, in many cases, only see the headlines from the last couple of weeks. You will want to get a more complete picture by viewing earlier headlines. This will only take a minute and will prevent you from making the wrong move.

For example, in August 2003, I passed on one of the stocks that came up in my search for the top percentage gainers. When I took the step of glancing at less recent headlines, I discovered a piece of worrisome news. Earlier in the summer, the NASDAQ had notified the company that it might be delisted, because its stock price failed to stay above NASDAQ's listing requirements.

When a stock is threatened with delisting, it suggests financial problems that may worsen later. Buying such a stock with the assumption that you could make a short-term profit is a risky decision.

When You Should Buy

How do you determine which point during the fall of a stock price is the most optimal time to buy? In other words, how do you know when the dip has reached the bottom, or close to it?

The answer to that question lies in looking for a steady increase in stock price, followed by a major retrenchment. Let's say, for instance, a company releases good news during pre-opening hours and the stock price quickly rises 20 percent. As profit-taking begins, the stock price comes off its high and attracts more and more buyers as it goes down. Assuming that the stock price is now only up by 10 percent—not that big of an increase by NASDAQ standards—it is likely that buyers will quickly outnumber sellers, therefore driving the price back up.

So, if the stock price was $5 before the news came out, then went up to $6, a good time to purchase it would be when the price goes down to $5.50. Why not wait until it goes below $5.50? Because of the good news, common sense tells you the stock won't lower much further, if at all.

Trading occurs at a fast pace, however, so watch carefully for these dips and peaks.

When You Should Sell

Once you've bought a stock on a dip, how do you know when to sell? Under normal circumstances, I recommend novice investors get out when they're up 10 percent for the day, and no more than 20 percent. The key is don't, I repeat, *don't* get greedy.

One exception to the 10 percent out rule is that occasion when a company's news is so positive that it gets an extraordinary amount of attention by the media and individual investors. The share price does not follow a dip and rise pattern, but rather continues to rise steadily for more than one day. If the price increase is supported by heavy volume, it may make sense to stay in the game. Among the NASDAQ percentage gainers I follow, I see this scenario of 100, 200, or 300 percent gains about once a month. I typically ride the wave through the first day, and sell on the following day at the beginning of regular market trading. This way, I keep my gains and sell before profit-taking becomes heavy, which often occurs at the opening of regular trading on the second day.

When Things Go Wrong

What happens when things go wrong? Let's say you bought on what you thought was the bottom, but the share price continues to drop. Perhaps the stock maintains its downward trend, despite a lack of new news. What can you do to minimize your losses?

Start by double-checking your research. Quickly visit the message boards, look at other companies in the industry, and review the overall news for the day. The market may have overreacted, and you may have overreacted with it. Or if there is truly good news, perhaps the stock will continue to go down for a while, then rebound.

A good rule of thumb is not to lose more than 10 percent of your purchase. It takes willpower to sell when you're down, but as it occurred during the technology bust of March 2000, sometimes stock prices, and the markets as a whole, just continue to fall. Don't be afraid to get out.

Many people are hesitant to sell at a loss, but if you've kept your trading buys to relatively small, conservative levels, you won't be losing much and you'll spare yourself a few gray hairs. Never panic. Simply keep your basic strategy in mind. Chances are very good that a loss you make one week will be recovered the next.

Chapter Eight

Strategy Number 3: Sympathy Plays

As you've noticed, how you apply (and whether you apply) the first two strategies depends on the time of day—the Last Hour of Trading versus pre-opening, for example. Here, I describe a strategy that often does not—the Sympathy Play strategy.

The sympathy play strategy is based on the concept that stocks of similar companies tend to react to events in similar ways. As you know, the stock market as a whole is made up of thousands of companies. Each company falls into what is known as a sector, or an industry group. While there are hundreds of industry groups, a dozen or so tend to get the most attention when it comes to trading activity. Examples of some major industry groups include technology, biotechnology, transportation, energy, and retail.

Investors tend to treat companies in a given industry group in the same way, even though the companies are, of course, entirely different. When news or rumors hit The Street that affect the share price of one company in an industry group, you'll often see the share prices of their competitors, or similar companies, move in the same direction. These are known as "sympathy moves."

An example of a common sympathy move often occurs with companies that are rumored to be takeover candidates. Let's say that a company like Microsoft is considering buying a security software company like Symantec.

In this type of scenario there might be resistance from Symantec's management and primary shareholders. In order to entice them to sell their shares, Microsoft may offer to pay a premium over the current market price. The very fact that a company has offered to pay a premium over the current price pushes up the price of Symantec's stock on the open market.

Before any of this actually occurs, however, rumors of the event hit The Street. In anticipation of a higher stock price, investors start buying shares of the takeover candidate, and the share price of Symantec increases as soon as the buzz hits The Street.

Almost simultaneously, the share prices of other security software companies also rise, as investors hypothesize that if Microsoft and Symantec are a good match, perhaps other similar companies might also be a good match. If the situation is a hostile takeover, the share prices will increase yet more dramatically because the acquiring company must typically offer even more of a premium for the shares of an unwilling candidate.

Another example of a sympathy play opportunity is when earnings announcements for a particular company are reported higher than expected. If Dell beats its expected earnings forecast, its share price will naturally rise. It is then very likely that the stock prices of Hewlett-Packard, IBM, and other computer manufacturers will also go up in anticipation that they may report good earnings as well.

A word of caution, however: stock prices typically go up *before* such positive news hits The Street, as professionals in the know buy shares on rumors. In order to take advantage of these types of Sympathy Plays, you need to have your ear to the ground and act very quickly.

A final illustration of the way in which Sympathy Plays make for good buying circumstances is in the example of American Airlines' fall from grace. In March 2003, rumors began swirling that American was in trouble financially, and the share price began to plummet, along with the share prices of nearly all the other major airlines. Many investors and analysts felt that bankruptcy was imminent for American and that its competitors might not be far behind.

Within six months, however, the CEO of American reduced the reputedly exorbitant compensation of its top executives and received salary concessions from its employees' key union negotiators. Bankruptcy rumors were supplanted by stability rumors, and American's shares began to rise. The stock price went from $2 in March to $10 in July. And once again, the shares of United, Delta, and other carriers followed suit. These bad news/ not so bad news scenarios happen every day in the market, and the watchful investor can do very well trading on the rumors.

Paying Attention to the Sectors

For the novice investor to be able to take advantage of Sympathy Plays, he or she must become familiar with the five or six major industry groups and the primary companies within those groups. Price increases on rumors happen fast, and you need to react very quickly if you want to profit from them.

If you're unfamiliar with the primary players in the major sectors and have not taken the time to research them, you may miss the opportunity to buy at the beginning of an upswing. If you miss the original upswing, you can still buy on a dip, although you may not realize as much gain.

How should you familiarize yourself with the sectors and the major companies within those sectors? Begin by choosing two or three industries and start paying attention to stocks that move in unison. Then try to always keep a real-time chart and quote window open on your screen for those stocks so that you can act quickly if the price of one of them changes.

Sympathy Plays are not limited to a few stocks within an industry. They can also apply to related industries. For example, in August 2003, the Northeastern region of the United States was subject to a huge power failure. This included major cities such as New York, Philadelphia, and Columbus, Ohio. Considered to be the most widespread blackout in U.S. history, it left 50 million people in the dark for more than 24 hours.

Eventually it became clear that the blackout was not due to a lack of electrical power, but to an aging power grid. This incident, however, prompted people to start thinking more seriously about alternative power sources such as fuel cells and solar power. The public's interest was, in turn, fueled further by the extensive coverage of alternative energy in the media and on message boards following the blackout. Subsequently, the share prices of alternative power companies rose in the weeks that followed. Not only were the alternative power companies affected, but also the shares of manufacturing companies who sold supplies and materials to the industry. Their share prices rose as well. Although nothing had changed in terms of each company's financial position—their income statement and balance sheets had remained the same— suddenly all of their share prices increased dramatically.

Keeping an Eye on the Future

While the *Lunchtime Millionaire* strategy focuses primarily on short-term market dynamics, it's always helpful to look to the future. Just as you watch individual stocks and segments to take advantage of Sympathy Plays, keep your eye on new technological advancements and constantly analyze how they might affect other industries in the long term. For example, the technology boom of the late 1990s affected not only technology firms, but companies like Federal Express, as investors believed the volume of shipping would increase because the amount of purchases being made online would increase. Even old economy companies like General Electric saw their stock increase in price as analysts projected their use of Internet technology would likely improve their profit margins.

The best way to find possible Sympathy Plays is to watch the news. As I discussed in chapter 4, the CNBC network is a particularly useful starting place for finding companies and industries on which to make a play. Because its coverage is so timely and broad, you'll get ideas nearly every day.

CHAPTER NINE

Placing Your Orders

O nce you've set up your online trading system, chosen your brokerage firm, and become familiar with basic investment tools and strategies, you're ready to place your first buy order. First, however, there are a few final details with which you'll want to familiar yourself:

1. The types of orders you can place

2. How to get the best execution of your orders

3. How to confirm your orders

4. The best methods of record keeping

TYPES OF ORDERS

There are two primary types of orders: market orders and limit orders. Each time you buy or sell a stock online, you're prompted to choose which type of order you'd like to place. The most common, a market order, specifies that you intend to buy the stock today, at the going market price.

On a normal market day, market orders are a relatively safe choice. Although placing a market order does not guarantee that your stock will be purchased at the price you see on your real-time quote screen, chances are very high that it will. These days, the markets are so liquid and orders are executed so quickly, there is typically little variation between the two prices.

The three instances when it is not safe to place a market order are:

1. When the stock you plan to buy is fluctuating widely in price

2. When the market is volatile overall

3. When you're dealing with stocks that have a high potential to be overly volatile, such as NASDAQ small cap stocks (generally stocks below $5 a share)

On the other hand, limit orders specify that you are only willing to buy a stock below, or at, a certain price. Limit orders therefore guarantee that you will not be affected if stock prices rise so rapidly that there is a noticeable difference between the price you saw on your real-time quote screen and the price at which you buy the stock. As a general rule, I nearly always place limit orders.

To illustrate how limit orders work, consider the following scenario: You've become interested in Authentidate Corporation, an authentication software company. The stock is currently trading at $10 a share, and you've just read that the company has recently landed a large government contract. You've checked your news sources and analyzed the short- and long-term charts. Based on your analysis, there is a good chance that the stock price will go up to $12 in the next 24 hours.

A 20 percent return is just what you're looking for, so you decide to place an order. You determine, however, that you won't pay more than $11 for the stock because, after commissions, the potential profit on the trade would not be worth the effort. Hence, you place a limit order specifying $11 as the maximum you're willing to pay. Chances are your order will actually be placed at the current market price of $10 a share, but you've protected yourself in case the price shoots up to $12 before your order is placed, and stays there.

Think of it this way: A limit order is a market order with a price ceiling or a price floor. What if you change your mind about the price at which you are willing to buy or sell? You can simply change your original order. Changing the limit price is simply a matter of visiting the "open orders" section on your brokerage account screen and clicking on the order you'd like to change. Nearly all brokerage firms allow this, and there are typically no additional commissions or fees for placing or changing limit orders. In addition, you can track these limit orders right on your regular open orders screen.

There are two caveats to placing limit orders. You should always choose as your limit the very highest price you are willing to pay. If you fail to do so, you may end up missing the boat entirely. Going back to Authentidate, if you were to set your limit order at slightly above the current price, say $10.25 a share, the price might shoot to $10.50 and you lose an opportunity to sell at $12, earning an 9 percent profit.

Such a missed opportunity doesn't mean you should keep raising your limit price, however. That is sometimes a temptation for investors, and it is called "chasing" stocks.

The key is to be patient. Frequently, a stock that has increased dramatically in price will drop soon afterward as investors sell and take their profits. This can provide a great second opportunity for you to purchase the stock as it falls below your limit. As additional investors jump in, the stock is likely to rise once again.

When it comes to the timeframe in which your market and limit orders will be executed, you have quite a bit of flexibility. In fact, there are four different types of market and limit orders:

- Good for the Day: Unless specified otherwise, these orders expire at the end of the same day's regular market hours.

- Good for the Day plus Extended Hours: As the title implies, these orders are good for both the regular trading session, and the after-market session (but do not include pre-market trading the next day). This is a fairly new alternative, which until recently was only available to institutional investors.

- Good Till Cancelled (GTC): These orders are active for three months or more, depending on the brokerage firm. They are only active during regular market hours.

- Good Till Cancelled Plus Extended Hours: These orders are a combination of the above two options. They can be executed anytime during regular market hours or extended market hours, for three months or more.

The option you choose will depend on your objectives for a particular trade. Here I summarize why you would choose (or not choose) each option.

- Good for the Day: Your interest in these orders doesn't go beyond today and you don't expect you'll need to participate in extended-hours trading. Besides, your brokerage firm may charge extra fees for extended hours trades and, in this case, you don't think it's worth paying those fees, which can range anywhere from 2 to 5 cents per share.

- Good for the Day plus Extended Hours: You know your stock is finishing strong and you want to give yourself a chance to own the stock at your chosen limit before it shoots up the next morning. As mentioned in chapter 6, many corporate earnings and news reports come out only after regular market hours have ended, so placing extended hours orders with limits can be very advantageous, even if extra fees apply.

- Good Till Cancelled (GTC): You know you're going to be away from your computer for a few days or more, but you don't want to miss the chance to buy the stock at a particular price. At the same time, you don't want to pay the extra fees, if they apply.

- Good Till Cancelled Plus Extended Hours: You want maximum flexibility. You've included the extra fees in your calculation. You'll make a profit.

Until now, we've discussed only buy orders. However, the rules on placing market and limit orders for selling are identical. When you place a sell order with a limit at a certain price, you are placing the order at the lowest price at which you're willing to sell.

Alternative Limit Strategy

An interesting tactic I sometimes use after I buy a stock is to place an immediate sell order with a limit so high that it seems unrealistic that anyone would purchase my shares. On rare occasions during after-market hours, a company will release dramatically unexpected news of earnings, product release, or corporate takeover that force the share price to spike up steeply. When that happens (and it is rare), I walk away with a tidy profit. Following is a hypothetical example:

Let's say that on March 3rd, I purchase 100 shares of SINA Corp. at $42, planning to sell it for $48 on March 4th. Then, before I stop trading for the day on March 3, I placed an order to sell at $65. That way if something unexpected should happen during after-hours trading, I would walk away with a handsome profit. By using this technique, I would give myself a chance to make a 50 percent return in just a few hours, instead of my usual 5 to 10 percent return.

If, on the other hand, no dramatic changes occur during after-hours trading, I simply wake up early the following morning and place a sell order with a more realistic limit. Please note that I only recommend using this tactic with stocks I plan to hold until the following morning. When I think it's wise to buy and sell a stock in a single day, I forego the strategy.

GETTING THE BEST EXECUTION

You may have heard talk of getting "good execution." Good execution means two things:

1. Your order will be filled at the best possible price.

2. Your order will be executed quickly.

GETTING THE BEST PRICE

Every brokerage firm has a variety of market makers with whom they work, and each market maker can buy or sell stocks at whatever price they choose (market makers are discussed in chapter 3. However, since brokerage houses are obligated to obtain the best price available for you, getting the best price should not be of concern to you.

That said, in a volatile market problems can occur with order execution on limit orders. When volume increases dramatically, some brokerage computer systems begin to slow down and orders are not executed as quickly. So if you are sitting on a limit order, you may miss your opportunity to buy or sell. As I demonstrated earlier, the price may move so quickly that it moves past your limit price before your order is filled.

SPEED OF EXECUTION

Most brokerages fill orders within ten seconds, and some, including firms like E*Trade, have guarantees that your order will be executed within nine seconds. If the trade is not executed within the specified time, some brokerages will waive the commissions on the order. Check with your brokerage customer service representative when opening an account. If your brokerage firm does not guarantee its execution speed, you may want to check Gomez.com and a couple of message boards to see what people say about its track record.

CONFIRMING YOUR TRADES

Immediately after you hit the send key when placing a trade online, a screen should appear confirming that your order has been placed. However, until you see that shares have either moved into or out of your account, you're not really sure. Even with the best brokerage firm trading systems, there are occasions when things will go wrong.

One example of a common trading error is when you place a trade without first making sure you have enough buying power. If you don't, the trade will be rejected, possibly without notice, and you may not discover what happened until you check your Trading History page.

To keep on top of your trading activities and nip any problems in the bud before things get too far along, take these three steps:

- After placing the trade, go to the brokerage's pending orders screen to look for the order.

- If the trade doesn't show on the pending orders screen, it may have been executed immediately, in which case it will appear on the portfolio screen.

- If the order doesn't show up on either the pending orders or the portfolio screen, visit the Trading History screen, where you will see the history of the transaction and whether it was cancelled due to a lack of buying power or some other issue.

It is important to note that no matter how good your brokerage firm's computer system may be, execution failures can occur when trading volume is very high. In that case, you'll typically get a message that the server is busy or has had a failure. Every brokerage firm includes a clause in its terms of service contract stating that it cannot be held responsible for errors due to busy servers or other technological failures. Hence, there is little you can do about a trade that didn't get executed for those reasons.

KEEPING RECORDS

Nearly all brokerage houses offer their clients the ability to access screens for keeping track of trades. You'll find Trading History, Portfolio Performance, and Account screens for just about everything you can think of.

However, I always recommend that investors keep a trading journal. Don't limit yourself to your brokerage house's activity and account screens. While the majority of brokerage screens are accurate, they are sometimes limited in how they display trades and activity.

For instance, most brokerage activity screens use one line for the buy trade and another line for the sell trade. You'll find it much easier to track your trades if you have both the buy and sell process for each trade on one line. I also recommend keeping a blank line under each trade just for you to note to yourself why you placed the trade and any lessons you learned or mistakes you made. This may seem like a lot of work but, as I will discuss in the next chapter, you will likely need this information later.

CHAPTER TEN

The Psychology of Trading

B uying and selling stocks can be very emotional. When you're up, it's easy to become overly confident. When you're down, it's just as natural to panic, and to take chances you wouldn't normally take. We are not machines, and our emotions sometimes overrule our good sense. But truly successful investors are those who recognize the psychology behind trading and know how to manage their emotions.

To be a successful investor, you must stay as calm, focused, and analytical as possible. This chapter is devoted to helping you maintain perspective, both when things go right and when things go wrong. In the pages that follow, I describe a number of mistakes that traders can make and psychological traps that they can fall into, and how you can avoid them.

MANAGING YOUR EMOTIONS:

10 TRADING DOS AND DON'TS

1. Do learn from history.

Perhaps the most dramatic event of our economic past is the boom and bust of the technology industry "bubble." What we experienced during the late 1990s can best be attributed to an extraordinary set of circumstances: over-optimism, unusually high capital spending, and extensive, and sometimes sensational, media coverage. These combined factors led to the kind of excitement and enthusiasm that prompted even the most conservative investors to transfer large quantities of their wealth into the stock market. As investors watched their friends' portfolios rapidly increase in value, they optimistically hopped on board. And many found themselves disappointed. Here are some lessons we can learn from this experience:

- No matter how "hot" a company seems to be, never invest blindly. Always do your homework and follow a strategy. I'm not recommending that you spend hours analyzing a company's financial statements. We are focusing on short-term strategies here. However, it's important to get a good feel for the company by researching the charts for the past year and the news for the past two weeks before placing a trade. Then, if everything looks safe, trust the momentum and go for it.

- When you make a decision to buy a stock, make it with the assumption that you'll be getting in and out within as little as one day. Remember that short-term investing is the cornerstone of the *Lunchtime Millionaire* strategy. Just as you have a strategy for when to buy, you must also have a strategy for when to sell, and that exit plan should be made as soon as you place the buy order.

For example, when you buy a stock at $5 a share, decide the optimal price at which you'll want to sell, then stick to that plan. Too often, beginning investors become overly optimistic and forget their original goal. As you watch a stock rise, it's tempting to put off selling and instead go along for the ride. This is what many people in the late 1990s did, losing hundreds of thousands of dollars. Rather than taking advantage of short-term rises and falls in stock prices, they were lulled into believing that prices would continue to rise indefinitely.

Yes, there may be instances where you feel compelled to sit on a stock for longer than a day, two days, or even a week. But if that is the case, remind yourself that you are then making a longer-term investment decision, and since you won't be selling the stock soon, you won't have those proceeds available for the next short-term opportunity.

2. Do learn the right way of taking a loss.

Of course, losing money is always painful. However, losses are an inevitable part of investing. They happen to everyone, even the best investors, at some time or another. Everyone makes mistakes, and learning from our mistakes is part of the process of becoming a successful investor.

In the movie *Wall Street,* the wealthy and powerful trader Gordon Gekko (played by Michael Douglas) explains his attitude about losses to a young broker by saying, "You win a few, you lose a few, but you keep on fighting." This statement sums up a large part of the psychology of trading. Your goal is to stay calm and focused when you're up and to remain calm and focused when you're down.

When you are trading stocks on a daily or weekly basis, it is extremely important to remain positive and not let yourself become discouraged by a bad trade. Over the years, I've followed one simple rule when it comes to trading losses: When I lose money on a trade, be it 5 percent or 10 percent, I just move on. Otherwise, I know that focusing on that loss may cause me to miss the next opportunity to make, for example, 30 or 50 percent on my next trade. Missing such an opportunity would be far worse that losing 5 or 10 percent on another.

That said, whenever you make a bad decision I recommend first taking a step back to analyze what happened. Understanding your mistakes or miscalculations will help your decision-making process in the future. Record your trading activity in your investment notebook, and always note the lessons you've learned. For example, when I experience a loss, I record the answers to the following questions:

- **Did I stick to my original strategy of selling at a particular price?** As I mentioned in the case of the technology boom and bust, the temptation to hold on just a little longer and make just a little more money can cause you to lose sight of you objectives.

- **Did I closely analyze the five-day chart?** As discussed in chapter 6, one strategy I recommend is to buy a stock that is showing a sudden increase in price and volume after three or four days of low volume and (relatively) flat price. Basically you want to make sure you are seeing true momentum, not just an accidental jump. When you look back, this might have been why the stock didn't go up further.

- **Did I properly analyze the news?** If I traded on good news, was the news really that noteworthy? For instance, a few months ago I came across a press release about an upcoming partnership between two software companies. The first part of the release seemed very positive in terms of what the partnership would bring to the smaller company. I jumped on the opportunity and quickly bought the smaller company's stock.

  When the stock price fell and I went back to the press release, I realized that the second part of the release contained information that tempered my initial optimism. I had been so eager to place a trade before the price got too high that I had glossed over the full details, reading only the positive aspects of the partnership.

3. Don't buy a stock that has risen more than 50 percent in the last few days.

It's human nature to want to join in when everyone else seems to be getting rich off a stock. This is the time, however, to be cautious. I can't stress this enough. If you're looking at a chart of a stock that has been going up constantly for a few days, it may be too late to buy.

Many investors bought the stocks when the price was still reasonable and, when they realize that they are making a 50 percent return or more, they will start cashing in, driving the stock price back down. Remember the Buying on a Dip strategy I talked about in chapter 7? Well, this is the time to wait for that dip.

4. Don't buy a stock when the spread is too high.

When the market for a particular stock is liquid (when there are a lot of buyers and sellers), the bid and ask prices are typically within one or two percentage points of each other. There are times, however, when the bid and ask prices will be farther apart. This usually occurs when the stock is not generating much interest from investors.

Now what if you bought such a stock and later realized that its price was not going in the upward direction you expected? Because the only price you can sell at (the bid price) is much lower than what you paid (because of the high spread), you will take an unfortunate loss.

5. Don't think that the stock price will double just because it's a penny stock.

Perception is a tricky thing, particularly when it comes to low-price stocks, or "penny stocks." What are penny stocks? Well, it depends whom you ask. Investors who trade in high-price stocks often refer to $1 or $2 stocks as penny stocks. Strictly speaking, however, penny stocks are stocks that sell for a few cents or less per share. The danger with penny stocks is that because they are so cheap, we tend to think of them as having more potential than they actually do.

Consider for example, two stocks. The first, Advanced Optics Electronics, which as of this writing is selling for one cent per share; the second, IBM, is selling for $88 per share. For Advanced Optics' stock price to go from one cent to one and a half cents in one day doesn't seem like much of a stretch, does it? But that's the equivalent of IBM's stock price, in one day, making the jump from $88 to $132 per share. You are, in essence, looking at two similar increases percentage-wise, but one seems pretty attainable while the other seems entirely unrealistic.

Because many investors hold this skewed perception, penny stocks do tend to increase in price rather dramatically, often within very short periods of time. But they can decrease in value just as quickly.

So never assume it's easy for a stock to go from one cent to two cents overnight. Give penny stocks the same careful thought and consideration you would give any other stock.

6. DON'T BE AFRAID TO TRADE DURING EXTENDED MARKET HOURS.

Many beginning investors shy away from pre- and post-market hours trading because they are unsure of the rules or the advantages of trading during these time periods. However, in reality, trading before or after regular market hours is just as easy as trading during regular market hours, and it can be very profitable. Just be aware of the following:

- Brokerage firms usually charge slightly higher commissions during pre/post-market hours. These fees may be in the neighborhood of a half cent per share or more. For instance, if you buy or sell $10,000 shares during after-hours trading, you'll likely pay an additional $50 commission on that trade.

- Spreads between the bid price and the ask price during extended trading hours are often higher because there are typically fewer market participants. However, if you buy or sell stocks that are in the top-ten list of most actives (in volume) you'll find there is virtually no difference.

7. Do take money off the table once in a while.

Throughout this book, I've emphasized the importance of starting with small trades, reinvesting your profits, and gradually using those reinvested funds to place larger trades. There will come a time in your trading activities, however, when you'll want to divert some of those profits into a long-term portfolio.

Taxes

When you sell stocks at a profit, you have to pay capital gains taxes. Typically, these gains are taxed at the same level as your regular income. Be sure to check with your accountant regarding the laws in your state, and with each successful trade, put aside a portion of your profits for taxes.

During the last week of December, you'll want to pay particular attention to your trades. Say, for example, that you happen to buy a stock that's fallen below the price at which you bought it. If you want that loss to decrease you tax obligations for the current year, you'll need to sell the stock before the close of the market on December 31.

8. DO TAKE BREAKS FROM TRADING.

Trading the markets is a fun and exciting hobby, but it's also one that requires concentration. And like anything that requires effort, it's important to take a break from it once in a while. Just as you head to the beach after a long year of work, taking a vacation from trading from time to time will increase your focus and enthusiasm when you return.

Sometimes the decision to take a break from trading will be prompted by other factors. For example, geopolitical crises often cause the markets to become jittery. During times like these, it's wise to carefully consider whether you want to be in the market, because there might not be sufficient momentum for you to buy and sell advantageously.

9. DON'T STOP DOING YOUR HOMEWORK.

One of the biggest thrills and yet one of the greatest dangers for a first-time trader is to score a major win with his or her first trade. Investors who make large profits coming out of the gate can get caught in the trap of becoming overly confident in their trading abilities. They may become less cautious and start taking risks. If you are fortunate (or unfortunate) enough to have this happen to you, force yourself to stay focused. Don't neglect your daily routine of monitoring the top ten NASDAQ stocks, analyzing the charts and news, checking the message boards, and watching CNBC.

10. Do keep yourself healthy.

Your trading success depends on it. Be sure to eat right, sleep well, and exercise regularly. You will feel better and you will make better trading decisions.

A Final Word

The reality for most of us is that we have to have a day job. We can't get in and out of stocks all day long like "day traders" do. Most of us don't want to become day traders anyway. That's just not our style.

We know that for the vast majority of people, get-rich-quick systems don't work. Common sense tells us that, short of winning the lottery or inheriting a fortune, we're not going to acquire a necessary level of savings overnight. We can't deal with a lot of risk either. We can't afford to.

The good news is that, with the combination of technology and the strategies I've described in this book, you can get to that level of comfort. Bit by bit, one trade at a time. And even have fun in the process.

Remember also that you don't have to invest your own money at the beginning. You can try the strategies on paper before you choose to get your feet wet.

This may be the end of this book, but as you dive into the world of online trading, I will continue to be at your side.

Bookmark my web site www.lunchtimemillionaire.com and regularly check back for additional investment tips and a regularly updated list of wireless trading -friendly venues.

I look forward to helping you reach your financial goals.

Glossary

This material is used by permission of Investopedia.com and by permission of John Wiley & Sons, Inc.

Above-The-Market: An order to buy or sell at a price set higher than the current market price of the security. *Investors may choose to place a limit order to sell, a stop order to buy, or a stop-limit order to buy.*

Advance/Decline Line (A/D): A technical analysis tool representing the total of differences between advances and declines of security prices. The advance/decline line is considered the best indicator of market movement as a whole. Stock indexes such as the DJIA only tell us the strength of thirty stocks whereas the A/D line provides much more insight.

After-Hours Trading: Trading after regular trading hours on the major exchanges. *This was once reserved for institutional investors, but now individuals may also trade after hours. Participation by market makers and ECNs is voluntary and, as a result, may offer less* *liquidity than normal hours of trading. If you are trading during pre-market or after-hours trading you should always use a limit order.*

American Stock Exchange (AMEX): Third most active market in the U.S., behind the NYSE and the Nasdaq. Most stocks traded on it are those of small- to mid-sized companies.

AMEX Composite Index: Index that measures the aggregate value of all AMEX-listed stocks.

Annual Report: Yearly report on a company's financial state and organization that is prepared by management for shareholders.

Antitrust Law: Any law that encourages competition by limiting unfair business practices and curbing the power of monopolies.

Appreciation: An increase in an asset's value.

Arbitrage: The simultaneous purchase and selling of a security in order to profit from a differential in the price. This usually takes place on different exchanges or marketplaces. *Also known as a riskless profit. An example of this is when an arbitrageur buys a stock on a foreign exchange that hasn't adjusted for the constantly changing exchange rate. The arbitrageur will purchase the undervalued stock and short sell the overvalued stock, thus profiting from the difference. This is recommended for experienced investors only.*

Ask: The price a seller is willing to accept for a security, also known as the offer price. *Sometimes called "the ask," this is the price the seller is asking for.*

Asset: Everything a company or individual owns or is owed.

Asset Allocation: Investment technique of dividing investment money among a variety of instruments and markets.

Asset-Management Accounts: All-in-one accounts that allow customers of brokerage firms to buy and sell securities and store cash in one or more money market mutual funds.

Auction Market: Trading securities on a stock exchange where buyers and sellers compete with other buyers and sellers for the best stock price. Trading in individual stocks is managed and kept orderly by a specialist.

Average Annual Yield: Measure of the return on investments of more than one year. It is calculated by adding each year's return on an investment and dividing that number by the number of years invested.

Bankruptcy: Legal process governed by the U.S. bankruptcy code for people or companies unable to meet financial obligations. Types of relief include Chapter 7 for liquidation, Chapter 11 for reorganization and repayment, and Chapter 13 for reorganization for individuals.

Bear Market: A market in which prices of a certain group of securities are falling or are expected to fall. Although figures can vary, a downturn of 15 to 20 percent or more in multiple indexes (Dow or S&P 500) is considered an entry into a bear market. *When you see a bear what do you do? Tuck in your arms and play dead! Fighting back can prove to be an extremely dangerous move. It is quite difficult for investors to make stellar gains during a bear market, unless they are short sellers.*

Bid: 1.) An offer made by an investor, trader, or dealer to buy a security. 2.) The price at which a market maker is willing to buy a security. *In other words, the bid is what someone is willing to pay for an asset.*

Bid-Ask Spread: The amount by which the ask price exceeds the bid.

Big Board: Another name for the New York Stock Exchange.

Block Order: An order submitted for the sale or purchase of a large quantity of securities. *In general, an order for 10,000 shares of stock (not including penny stocks) is considered a block order.*

Block Trade: The sale or purchase of a large quantity of securities. *In general, 10,000 shares of stock (not including penny stocks) or $200,000 worth of bonds is considered a block trade.*

Blue Chip Stocks: Stock of a well-established and financially-sound company that has demonstrated its ability to pay dividends in both good and bad times. *These stocks are usually less risky than other stocks. The stock price of a blue chip usually closely follows the S&P 500.*

Book Value: A company's net worth (difference between a company's assets and its liabilities).

Bottom Fishing: Buying stocks whose prices have bottomed out or fallen to low levels.

Bull Market: A market in which prices of a certain group of securities are rising or are expected to rise. *Wall Street couldn't be happier during a bull market. Typically, this is a period of optimism in the market.*

Capital Gain: Difference between the purchase price and the sale price of an asset when the asset was sold for more than it was bought. Opposite of a capital loss.

Chartered Financial Analyst (CFA): The best-known financial designation, given to qualifying planners by the CFP Board of Standards.

Chicago Board of Trade (CBOT): One of the oldest futures exchanges, where agricultural and financial futures are traded.

Chicago Board Options Exchange (CBOE): An exchange set up by the Chicago Board of Trade to trade stock options.

Churning: Excessive trading in a customer's brokerage account, done to generate increased commission income. Churning is a securities law violation.

Circuit Breaker: Refers to any number of measures that can be used by stock exchanges during large selloffs. After an index has fallen a certain percentage, actions such as trading halts or restrictions on program trading can be taken. Sometimes called a "collar."

Close: The end of a trading session. The closing price is what's quoted in the newspaper. *The closing of the NYSE is marked with a bell.*

Close Position: Getting out of a position in a particular stock or security. *If a broker recommends that you close your long position on a stock, she means "sell it immediately."*

Closely Held: Companies in which stock and voting control are concentrated in the hands of a few investors, although the companies' shares may be traded to a limited extent.

Closing Price: The last traded price of a stock when the market closes.

Commodities: Bulk goods, such as grains, metals, livestock, oil, cotton, coffee, sugar, and cocoa that are sold on the commodities exchanges in the form of futures contracts.

Common Stock: Represents part ownership of a company. Holders of common stock have voting rights but no guarantee of dividend payments.

Composite Trading: Total amount of trading across markets in a share that is listed on the NYSE or the AMEX. This includes transactions on those exchanges, the five regional exchanges, and on the Nasdaq.

Confirmation: The written acknowledgment provided by a broker indicating that a trade has been completed. It includes details such as the date, price, commission, fees, settlement terms, and so on.

Consumer Credit: Money loaned to individuals, usually on an unsecured basis, requiring monthly repayment. Bank loans, credit cards, and installment credit are examples of consumer credit.

Consumer Price Index: A gauge of inflation that measures changes in the prices of consumer goods. The index is based on a list of specific goods and services purchased in urban areas. It is released monthly by the Labor Department.

Correction: A reverse movement, usually downward, in the price of an individual stock, bond, commodity, index, or the stock market as a whole.

Cost Basis: In accounting, the valuation of an asset that includes the cost of the asset and factors in items like depreciation, capital gains, and dividends.

Cost-Push Inflation: A sustained rise in prices caused by businesses passing on increases in costs, especially labor costs, to purchasers.

Curbs In: An indication that trading curbs have been installed on the New York Stock Exchange.

Cyclical Stock: Used to describe a stock that rises quickly when economic growth is strong, and falls rapidly when growth is slowing down. *An example is the automobile market, because as growth slows in the economy, consumers have less money to spend on new cars. Non-cyclical stocks would be in industries like health care, for which there is constant demand.*

Day Order: Any order to buy or sell a security that automatically expires if not executed on the day the order is placed. *A day order will not be executed if the limit or stop order prices were not met during the day. A way to increase the life of an order is to order securities on a "good 'til cancelled" basis, where, as the name implies, the trade will not expire until it is cancelled or until it reaches a maximum time limit set by the brokerage.*

Debt: Securities such as bonds, notes, mortgages, and other forms of paper that indicate the intent to repay an amount owed.

Default: Failure to pay principal or interest on a financial obligation. It can also refer to a breach or nonperformance of the terms of a debt instrument.

Defensive Securities: Stock of companies whose earnings tend to grow despite the business cycle, like food and drug firms, or of companies that pay relatively high dividends, like utilities.

Deflation: A decline in the general price level of goods and services that results in increased purchasing power of money. The opposite of inflation.

Depression: A severe downturn in an economy that is marked by falling prices, reduced purchasing power, and high unemployment.

Derivative: A financial product whose value is derived from an underlying financial asset, such as stocks, bonds, currencies, or mortgages. Derivatives may be listed on exchanges or traded privately over-the-counter. For example, derivatives may be futures, options, or mortgage-back securities.

Discount Brokers: Brokers who charge lower commissions than full-service brokers and usually limit their service to trade execution.

Discount Rate: The interest rate charged by the Federal Reserve on loans to banks.

Disinflation: A slowdown in the rate of price increases. Disinflation occurs during a recession, when sales drop and retailers are unable to pass higher prices along to consumers.

Diversification: Spreading investments among different types of securities to lessen risk.

Dividend: A cash payment, using profits, announced by a company's board of directors and distributed among stockholders. Dividends may be in the form of cash, stock, or property. All dividends must be declared by the board of directors.

Dividend Yield: A company's annual dividend expressed as a percentage of current stock price.

Dollar-Cost Averaging: A strategy to invest fixed amounts of money in securities at regular intervals, regardless of the market's movements.

Double-Dip Recession: When the gross domestic product (GDP) growth slides back to negative after a quarter or two of brief positive growth. In other words, a recession followed by a short-lived recovery, followed by another recession.

Dow Jones Averages: There are four Dow Jones Averages that track prices changes in various sectors. The Dow Jones Industrial Average tracks the price changes of the stock of thirty industrial companies. The Dow Jones Transportation Average monitors the price changes of the stocks of twenty airlines, railroads, and trucking companies. The Dow Jones Utility Average measures the performance of the stock of fifteen gas, electric and power companies. The Dow Jones sixty-five Composite Average monitors the stock of all sixty-five companies that make up the other three averages.

Dow Jones Equity Market Index: Index that measures price changes in more than one hundred U.S. industry groups. The stocks in the index represent about 80 percent of U.S. market capitalization and trade on the NYSE, the AMEX, and the Nasdaq. The index is capitalization weighted.

Dow Jones Global Indexes: Some 2,700 companies' stocks in twenty-nine countries worldwide are tracked by geographic region and by 120 industry groups.

Dow Jones Industrial Average (DJIA): Often referred to as the Dow, this is the best known and most widely reported indicator of the stock market's performance. The Dow tracks the price changes of thirty mostly industrial stocks traded on the NYSE.

Their combined market value is roughly equal to 20 percent of the market value of all U.S. stocks and 25 percent of those listed on the NYSE.

Dow Jones World Stock Index: An index that measures the performance of more than 2,000 companies worldwide that represent more than 80 percent of the equity capital on twenty-five stock markets.

Downside Risk: An estimation of a security's potential to suffer a decline in price if the market conditions turn bad. *You can think of this as an estimate of the amount that you could lose on a stock or other investment.*

Earnings: Income after a company's taxes and all other expenses have been paid. Also called profit or net income.

Earnings Per Share: The amount of earnings allocated to each share of common stock. Calculated by dividing earnings by the number of shares outstanding.

Earnings Yield: A company's per-share earnings expressed as a percentage of its stock price. This provides a yardstick for comparing stocks with bonds, as well as with other stocks.

Electronic Communications Network (ECN): An electronic system that attempts to eliminate third party orders entered by an exchange market maker or an over-the-counter (OTC) market maker, and permits such orders to be executed either in whole or in part. *An ECN connects major brokerages and individual traders so that they can trade directly among themselves without having to go through a middleman.*

Economic Indicators: Key statistics used to analyze business conditions and make forecasts.

Emerging Markets: Financial markets in nations that are developing market-based economies, such as in Latin America and China.

Equity: In the securities markets, it is the part of a company's net worth that belongs to shareholders.

Euro: The currency of the twelve countries in the new European Union.

Eurodollars: Dollar-denominated deposits in banks outside the U.S.

European Union: An international governmental organization of fifteen Western European nations created in December 1991 with its own institutional structures and decision-making framework.

Exchange: A centralized place for trading securities and commodities, usually involving an auction process.

Ex-Date: The date on or after which a security is traded without a previously declared dividend or distribution. After the ex-date, a stock is said to trade ex-dividend. *This is the date on which the seller, and not the buyer, of a stock will be entitled to a recently announced dividend. The ex-date is usually two business days before the record date. It is indicated in newspaper listings with an X.*

Federal Debt: The amount of debt sold by the federal government to fund past deficits.

Federal Deficit: Money owed by the federal government when spending exceeds tax revenues collected.

Federal Funds Rate: The interest rate banks charge on overnight loans to banks that need more cash to meet bank reserve requirements. The Federal Reserve sets the interest rate.

Federal Reserve: The central bank of the U.S. that sets monetary policy. The Federal Reserve oversees money supply, interest rates, and credit with the goal of keeping the U.S. economy and currency stable. Governed by a seven-member board, the system includes 132 regional Federal Reserve Banks, twenty-five branches, and all national and state banks that are part of the system. Also called the Fed.

Flight To Quality: When the gross domestic product (GDP) growth slides back to negative after a quarter or two of brief positive growth. In other words, a recession followed by a short-lived recovery, followed by another recession.

Float: The total number of shares publicly owned and available for trading. The float is calculated by subtracting restricted shares from outstanding shares. *For example, a company may have 10 million outstanding shares, but only 7 million are trading on the stock market. So, the float would be 7 million. Stocks with small floats, less than 3 million shares, tend to be a lot more volatile than others.*

Full Service Broker: A broker that provides a large variety of services to its clients. These services include research and advice, retirement planning, tax tips, and much more. Of course, this all comes at a price, as commissions at full-service brokerages are much higher than at discount brokerages.

Good This Month (GTM): A limit order placed with a broker that will last until the end of the current month. *If the order is not filled before the end of the month, it will expire.*

Initial Public Offering: The first sale of stock by a private company to the public. IPOs are often smaller, younger companies seeking capital to expand their business.

Insider: Any person who has or has access to valuable nonpublic information about a corporation. *Examples of an insider are the directors and officers of a company. The stockholders who own more than 10 percent of equity in a company are also insiders.*

Large Cap (Big Cap): Companies having a market capitalization between $10 billion and $200 billion. *Keep in mind that classifications such as "large cap" and "small cap" are only approximations that change over time. Also, the exact definition can vary between brokerage houses.*

Level Two: A trading service consisting of real-time access to the quotations of individual market makers registered in every Nasdaq-listed security, as well as market makers' quotes in OTC Bulletin Board securities. *This allows you to watch the trades being executed right in front of you. Also known as Level II.*

Limit Order: An order placed with a brokerage to buy or sell a predetermined amount of shares at a specified price or better than the specified price. Limit orders also allow an investor to limit the length of time an order can be outstanding before cancelled. *Limit orders are especially useful on a low-volume or highly volatile stock.*

Liquidity: The degree to which an asset or security can be bought or sold in the market without affecting the asset's price. Liquidity is characterized by a high level of trading activity. *Examples of assets with good liquidity include blue chip common stock and those assets in the money market.*

Margin: 1.) The use of borrowed money to purchase securities, referred to as "buying on margin." 2.) The amount of equity contributed by a customer as a percentage of the current market value of the securities held in a margin account.

Margin Call: A demand that an investor using margin deposit additional money or securities to bring a margin account up to the minimum maintenance margin. *A broker will make a margin call if one or more of the securities you have bought (with borrowed money) decreases in value past a certain point. You will be forced to either deposit more money in the account or sell off some of your assets. This is sometimes called a fed call.*

Margin Maintenance: The amount of equity that must be maintained in a margin account. *After securities have been bought on margin, the NYSE and the NASD require that the level of margin be maintained at 25 percent of the total market value of the securities in the margin account. Keep in mind that this level is a minimum and many brokerages have higher maintenance requirements of 30 to 40 percent.*

Market Order: An order to buy or sell a stock immediately at the best available current price. A market order guarantees execution. Often this type of order has low commissions due to the minimal work brokers need to do.

Mid Cap: Short for "middle cap," mid cap refers to stocks with a market capitalization of between $2 billion to $10 billion. *Keep in mind that classifications such as "large cap" and "small cap" are only approximations that change over time. Also, the exact definition can vary between brokerage houses.*

Momentum: The rate of acceleration of a security's price or volume. *Once a momentum trader sees an acceleration in a stock's price, earnings, or revenues, the trader will often take a long or short position in the stock with the hope that its momentum will continue in either an upward or downward direction. This strategy relies more on* *short-term movements in price rather then fundamental particulars of companies.*

Moving Average Chart: Frequently used in technical analysis, a moving average is an indicator that shows the average value of a security's price over a period of time. When calculating, you need to specify the time span, i.e. 200 days. *Moving averages are used to emphasize the direction of a trend and to smooth out price and volume fluctuations or "noise" that can confuse interpretation.*

Overbought: In technical analysis, it is a market in which the volume of buying that has occurred is greater than the fundamentals justify.

Oversold: In technical analysis, it is a market in which the volume of selling that has occurred is greater than the fundamentals justify.

Odd Lot: An amount of a security that is less than the normal unit of trading for that particular security. *For stocks, any transaction less than 100 shares is usually considered to be an odd lot.*

Open Order: An order to buy or sell a security that remains in effect until it is either canceled by the customer or executed. *Open orders commonly occur when investors place price restrictions on their buy and sell transactions. As market orders are filled instantaneously, investors who enter limit orders will typically have to wait before the price that they set as their limit is reached. These orders will remain open either for the duration determined by the customer or until they are filled.*

Over-The-Counter (OTC): A security which is not traded on an exchange, usually due to an inability to meet listing requirements. For such securities, brokers/dealers negotiate directly with one another over computer networks and by phone. The NASD carefully monitors their activities. *The Nasdaq is considered to be an OTC market, with the tier one being represented by companies such as Microsoft, Dell, and Intel. Be very wary of some OTC stocks, the OTCBB (Bulletin Board) stocks are either penny stocks or hold bad credit records.*

Over-The-Counter Bulletin Board (OTCBB): An electronic trading service offered by the NASD. Traditionally home to many small and micro cap companies, it is considered very high risk.

Outstanding Shares: The number of shares that are currently owned by investors. This includes restricted shares (shares owned by the company's officers and insiders) and shares held by the public. Shares that the company has repurchased are not considered outstanding stock. *This number is more important than the authorized shares or float. It is used in the calculation of many metrics including market capitalization and EPS.*

Penny Stock: A stock that sells for less than $1 a share but may also rise to as much as $10/share as a result of heavy promotion. All penny stocks are traded OTC or on the Pink Sheets.

Pre-Market: Trading done before the regular market opens. *Participation by market makers and ECNs is voluntary, and, consequently, there may be less liquidity than during normal hours of trading.*

Program Trading: Computerized trading used primarily by institutional investors, typically for large volume trades. Orders from the trader's computer are entered directly into the market's computer system and executed automatically. *Program trades are usually executed if index prices sink or rise to a certain level. This tends to create very volatile situations and, as a result, there are restrictions on when program trading can be used.*

Pump and Dump: A highly unethical practice occurring mainly on the ternet. A small group of informed people buy a stock before they recommend it to thousands of investors. The result is a quick spike in the price followed by an equally quick downfall. The people who bought the stock early sell off when the price peaks.

Quantitative Analysis: A security analysis that uses financial information derived from company annual reports and income statements to evaluate an investment decision.

Resistance: The price a stock or market can trade at, but cannot exceed, for a certain period of time. Often referred to as resistance level.

Reverse Split: A reduction in the number of a corporation's shares outstanding that increases the par value of its stock or its earnings per share. The market value of the total number of shares (market capitalization) remains the same. *For example, a 1:2 reverse split means you get half as many shares, but at twice the price.*

Risk: The chance that an investment's actual return will be different than expected. This includes the possibility of losing some or all of the original investment. It is usually measured using the historical returns or average returns for a specific investment.

Round Lot: The normal unit of trading for a security, which is generally 100 shares of stock. *Anything less than 100 shares is considered an odd lot.*

Selling Short: The selling of a security that the seller does not own, or any sale that is completed by the delivery of a security borrowed by the seller. Short sellers assume that they will be able to buy the stock at a lower amount than the price at which they sold short. *This is an advanced trading strategy with many unique risks and pitfalls.*

Share Repurchase: A company's plan to buy back its own shares from the marketplace, reducing the number of outstanding shares. Typically, this is an indication that the company's management thinks the shares are undervalued.

Sideways Market: A situation in which stock price changes little over a period of time. *Consequently, traders who follow trends when making their investment decisions will tend to perform poorly during a sideways market. Also known as "horizontal price movement" or "flat market."*

Stock Split: The division of a company's existing stock into more shares. In a 2-for-1 split, each stockholder would receive an additional share for each share formerly held. *This is usually a good indicator that a company's share price is doing well. However, you don't get any more value, just twice as many shares.*

Stop Limit Order: An order placed with a broker to buy or sell at a specified price (or better) after a given stop price has been reached or passed. *Stop limit orders are used to buy a stock when it reaches a certain price, this allows investors to buy when the stock has upward momentum behind it.*

Stop Loss Order: An order placed with a broker to sell when a certain price is reached. It is designed to limit an investor's loss on a security position. This is sometimes called a stop market order. *In other words, setting a stop loss order for 10 percent below what you bought the stock for would limit your loss to 10 percent.*

Stop Order: An order to sell a stock when its price falls to a particular point, thus limiting an investor's loss (or locking in a profit). Also referred to as a stop-loss order. *Investors commonly use a stop order before leaving for holidays or entering a situation where they will be unable to monitor their portfolio for an extended period of time.*

Technical Analysis: A method of evaluating securities by analyzing statistics generated by market activity, such as past prices and volume. Technical analysts do not attempt to measure a security's intrinsic value but rather use charts to identify patterns that can suggest future activity.

Trend: The general direction of the price of an asset or market in general.

Tick: The minimum upward or downward movement in the price of a security. *Historically, stocks didn't trade in decimals. A stock would move in amounts of 1/8, 1/16, or 1/32 of a dollar (the tick). This changed when the decimal system was introduced.*

Undervalued: A stock or other security that is trading below its true value. *Analysts will usually recommend an undervalued stock with a strong buy rating.*

Value Stock: A stock that is considered undervalued by a value investor. Common characteristics of such stocks include a high dividend yield and low price-to-book ratio.

Volume: The number of shares or contracts traded in a security or an entire market during a given period. *Typically, a large increase in volume means that some sort of news is coming out. Volume is a very important indicator in technical analysis.*

Warrant: A derivative security that gives the holder the right to purchase securities (usually equity) from the issuer at a specific price within a certain time frame. *The main difference between warrants and call options is that warrants are issued and guaranteed by the company, whereas options are exchange instruments and not issued by the company. Also, the lifetime of a warrant is often measured in years, while the lifetime of a typical option is months.*

Index

Y

ACKNOWLEDGMENTS

Many people were instrumental in bringing this book to completion.

Heartfelt thanks go to Jennifer Koretz for her unconditional support, astute content suggestions, and extensive research assistance, and to Jane Riley, whose encouragement throughout the process of writing this book was deeply appreciated.

To the following, I also offer my deepest gratitude.

To Diana DeLonzor, in particular, for her hard work in helping me take the book to the next level and for all her invaluable insight along the way. To Mike O'Sullivan, for his expert critical eye and for his input on many aspects of this project. To Meghan Ward, my exceptional copyeditor.

To Andy Heller, for his contribution to the title of the book. To my talented photographer, Amanda Koerner. Many thanks also go to Jerry Irvin and Romanus Wolter, whose input greatly helped clarify my thinking.

Finally, my thanks go to my "Quality Assurance" team, Lindsay Helseth and Emerald Bloom.

Special thanks go to:

WEBOPEDIA.COM for its permission to republish some of the computer terms defined on its website: www.webopedia.com

INVESTOPEDIA.COM for their permission to republish some of the financial terms defined on their website: www.investopedia.com

John Wiley & Sons, Inc for their permission to republish some of the financial terms defined in the book CNBC/CNBC GUIDE TO MONEY AND MARKETS by Jeff Wuorio. Copyright © 2002 by CNBC.

Yahoo! for its screen shots, stock screener and charts from the financial website Yahoo! Finance: finance.yahoo.com Copyright © 2002-2004 by Yahoo!

About the Author

Didier Perennez has more than twenty years of experience in business, education, software development, and the stock market. He has served as lead software engineer and consultant for portfolio managers and financial software companies both in Europe and the United States.

Didier teaches people how to use technology and low-risk strategies to get closer to their financial goals more quickly. He is a financial consultant, author, and speaker who has placed thousands of stock trades.